The Stories We Live

The Stories We Live

Finding God's Calling
All around Us

KATHLEEN A. CAHALAN

William B. Eerdmans Publishing Company
Grand Rapids, Michigan

Wm. B. Eerdmans Publishing Co.
2140 Oak Industrial Drive NE, Grand Rapids, Michigan 49505
www.eerdmans.com

23 22 21 20 19 18 17   1 2 3 4 5 6 7

ISBN 978-0-8028-7419-1

Library of Congress Cataloging-in-Publication Data

Names: Cahalan, Kathleen A., author.
Title: The stories we live : finding God's calling all around us /
    Kathleen A. Cahalan.
Description: Grand Rapids : Eerdmans Publishing Co., 2017. | Includes
    bibliographical references.
Identifiers: LCCN 2016046035 | ISBN 9780802874191 (pbk.: alk. paper)
Subjects: LCSH: Vocation—Christianity. | Storytelling—Religious
    aspects—Christianity.
Classification: LCC BV4740 .C28 2017 | DDC 248.4—dc23
    LC record available at https://lccn.loc.gov/2016046035

In thanksgiving for Margaret O'Gara (1947–2012)

and her many callings:

theologian, teacher, reformer,

wife, friend, ecumenist,

and Collegeville Institute board member

Contents

Introduction

"I don't know that I've ever been given a calling."

Do you think you've ever been given a calling? How would you describe the journey that has brought you to where you are today? What gives your life purpose, meaning, and joy? What are your passions? Your questions? Your challenges? Where is God in your story?

When I asked Jay about his life's journey, he described the joy of family life, his skills as a financial analyst, and the meaning he gets from helping others with difficult decisions. He found God in others, in leadership and coaching, and especially in his role as father and husband. Jay was grateful for his life, and he wanted to give back to the community. I asked him, "Do you have a sense that God has called you to be a father, coach, banker, and community member?" "Well," he said, "I don't know that I've ever been given a calling."

I've heard Jay's story many times from people in churches, students in classrooms, friends, and even strangers. God's callings are all around us, but we don't always see them. Jay's life is an example of what Christians have traditionally called "vocation." (The word "vocation" has the same meaning as "calling"; it comes from the Latin *vocare*, which means "to call.") He strives to follow the gospel; he engages in meaningful work that is a service to others; he has a sense of his capacities and gifts; he is committed to his family as parent and spouse; and he wants to give his life for the sake of his neighbors and community. Listening to his story, I wanted to cry out, "Jay, you've been given many callings!" But he wasn't able to see this yet.

What would change and deepen for Jay if he started to see his life's relationships and work as callings from God? How might your life change if you started to see this too? It matters if the story we tell about our lives is rooted in God's callings. But how do we tell our stories? What language can we use to capture the callings that make up our lives?

"Prep-o-si-tion. noun, grammar: A class of words found in many languages that express relationship"

Here's one way people commonly talk about their callings. They use a noun: "I'm trying to figure out what my *vocation* is" or "I'm searching for the *meaning* of my life." The danger is that when you speak of vocation as a noun, it can sound as if it is something already constructed. God will hand it to you ready-made. But life is rarely that neat and tidy. Speaking of your callings with nouns ends up sounding static, passive, and singular.

There's another, more active way to frame your calling: as a verb. For instance, in my life, God has been known to call out to me, sometimes in a whisper, but mostly by a shout, a nag, or a push. I've been known to holler back. Verbs are dynamic; they create action and movement in a story. When we describe the action of our lives, we can begin to see that callings are a response to God and others.

But another kind of word explores vocation even better: prepositions. They are parts of speech that connect words to other words: to the store, with Ed, away from barking dogs, for milk. Prepositions express relationship. When we frame vocation through prepositions, callings become more relational, dynamic, and multiple. Prepositions express the whole of our lives, even the places and experiences we never thought of as callings. In this short book, I use eight prepositions to explore vocation as a relationship between our lives and God's purposes:

I am called
by God,
to follow,
as I am,
from grief,
for service,
in suffering,
through others,
within God.

Each of these prepositions reveals a different dimension of our callings. We are called *by* God, who is the source of our callings. We are called *to* follow the way shown by Jesus and taken up by his disciples; this calling we share with each other. We are called *as* unique persons with a particular history and circumstance. We are called *from* the losses and grief we suffer over time, so that we can embrace life again. We are called to give our lives *for* others, not simply for our self-improvement or fulfillment. We are even called in our deepest suffering to carry out God's purposes in mysterious ways. We are called through the people in our lives, because vocation takes root in community. And, finally, we are called together to live within God's loving embrace, both now and in the life to come.

Prepositions, the smallest words in our vocabulary, carry the meaning of our callings in the stories we tell. By shifting the grammar of vocation, prepositions will help us see God at work in our own life, where God is inviting us to find our story within the divine story.

What is your story? How have you experienced being called by God? If you have, what difference has it made for you and others? If you haven't, what might happen if you started to see your life as a story of callings? Throughout this book, I share many stories of callings from a variety of perspectives. Many were told to me by people in churches; some come from my own life. My hope is that hearing and reflecting on these stories will give you a broader sense of the meaning of vocation and invite you to discover God's purposes in your life. There is no single or right way of speaking about our callings. Nouns, verbs, and prepositions are all necessary to storytelling. We find our callings within the stories of our lives—the story of God at work all *around* us. That would add another preposition to the list.

CHAPTER 1

Called by God in Multiple Ways

Three ways of talking about being called

Remember a time when you felt God at work in your life. What did you learn from this experience? A calling by God can come in any number of ways. Think of different times, places, or circumstances that you felt God's presence, nudge, or invitation. There is no single way in which God calls us—though we sometimes get hung up with certain expectations about how God calls. Have you had Paul's blinding experience on the road to Damascus? I haven't. If you think that is the only way God reaches out to people, you might easily get discouraged.

We often do not pay attention to our own experiences, as ordinary as they might be. Could God be calling you by conversations with other people? Or by trying out a different job and area of study? Could God be inviting you by helping you to realize what you don't want to do? Have you ever seen God's hand at work by looking back at your life?

To understand the mysterious ways God works in our lives, consider three experiences or images for the ways God calls us: the plan, the pilgrimage, and the surprising "aha!" moment. Many of us believe and hope that God has a plan for our lives and we can figure it out. Many want to find the right path to follow. And some people, regardless of plan or path, awaken to a surprising realization. These are three possible ways we can talk about being called by God that connect us to both the biblical stories and the stories we live.

"For surely I know the plans I have for you, says the LORD, *plans for your welfare and not for harm, to give you a future with hope." (Jeremiah 29:11)*

Have you ever wondered if God had a plan for your life? Many Christians have believed that God's call means that God has a highly detailed, exact plan for their life, and that vocation consists in figuring out that plan. Such belief expresses a deep faith that God is all-knowing and cares about the very details of your life (e.g., "even the hairs of your head are all counted" [Luke 12:7]). But for some, this claim has been hard to believe. If God has a plan, does it include Hurricane Katrina, a child's illness, or the Iraq War? Some kinds of suffering and pain make no sense if God is all-knowing and has an exact plan for every detail of history, including the details of your life. Furthermore, if there is a plan, do you have any choice in what you do?

When it comes to the language of vocation, the idea of God as the divine planner may be one of the most challenging ideas about vocation. As with any image of God, there is a truth at the heart of this claim. Consider the early days of the Israelites' experience of being saved from slavery and given the hope of a promised land. Over time, they came to realize that God had intentions, direction, and purposes for them. But they also had to embrace the mystery of God's plan, especially when they found themselves in the wilderness for a long time. Part of the plan seemed to include how they would respond to the struggles along the way.

One problem with seeking out a specific plan is that it creates anxiety that you might miss your one chance to get it right, that figuring out your vocation is a high-stakes scavenger hunt where you are searching for one hidden treasure. Young adults who are in college, in particular, think that vocation is choosing the right major that prepares them for a career or that a "right person" is out there to be their partner. "I always thought God had a plan for me, but now I'm not sure," said Leslie, a college sophomore. "I'm so confused because now there doesn't seem like a plan, or I just can't find it." Leslie had a plan to study theater, but she did not enjoy it. She felt bad, wondering if it was unfaithful to try something else. She started taking management courses in the hopes that she could work in a nonprofit agency. In fact, she had to take up some other interests in order to figure out the plan, but giving up theater was certainly not a failure of the plan. God may be inviting Leslie to try out any number of possibilities so that she can find what best fits her. What if that invitation is God's plan? The most faithful thing in her situation may have been trying something new.

Figuring out a plan for our lives is not a new problem for the Christian faith. Consider what God says when speaking through Jeremiah: "For surely I know the plans I have for you, says the LORD, plans for your welfare and not for harm, to give you a future with hope" (Jer. 29:11). In fact, "you" here is plural. God is speaking to and about the whole community—not one

4

individual. God's plan is the same for all of us: to live and work for the sake of God's mission in the world. Perhaps God's plan for us as the people of God is to create our lives according to the divine purposes and participate in life-giving ways for each other. In that sense, God's plan is about creating, making, restoring, mending, uniting, connecting, healing, and correcting all that stands opposed to God's ways and purposes.

Perhaps a more helpful way is to say that God does not create you *with* a vocation (one single plan that God has made), but with the capacity for vocations (the ability to engage in dialogue with God and others to create a plan for your life). Vocation becomes, then, a creative act, something we create with God and others, unique to each of our lives.

When I ask people about their story of calling, a few say they experience God's call as a precise plan, or at least have had a strong sense from childhood that God has called them to a particular role, job, relationship, or gift. Something has been given to them to do. Margaret, the woman I dedicated this book to, was a child when she experienced a call to reform the church. She felt her vocation was more like an acorn. Her life could only become one thing—an oak tree, or, in her case, a reformer. She had this sense of calling all her life until she died. But even this certainty did not make the calling any easier, since hers was a service filled with heartache and struggle at times. If you have the experience, like Margaret, that there is a definite plan, you know what I mean. If you don't have this experience, don't worry. God may be working in your life in a different way.

The way is made by walking.

Many people do not experience God's call with the precision that Margaret did. They find that life's callings are more like a journey. Many people describe their vocations as a pilgrimage, a journey, even an exile—all biblical ways of describing walking with others and with God. Throughout history the pilgrim was a "traveler," "one who had come from afar," usually on foot, traveling to holy places seeking healing and guidance. The pilgrim set out on the journey as an act of devotion, penance, and love for God.

Abraham was called as a pilgrim. "By faith Abraham obeyed when he was called to set out for a place ... and he set out, not knowing where he was going" (Heb. 11:8). Pilgrims experience a call to follow a particular way and trust that what they need will emerge as part of the journey. But they must walk to figure it out: to learn as they go, to struggle under difficulty, and even to fail at times. By doing so they discover hospitality, the need to lighten their bag by discarding items, and to be open to the unexpected. As a pilgrim on the Camino de Santiago (the Way of Saint James), the popular pilgrimage in Spain, theologian and pastor Arthur Boers discovered that "the Way commended by Christ has to be journeyed; it is made by walking."

Even on pilgrimage, we may set out with a map and a destination, but by walking the way each day we learn that our plans can be quickly disrupted. We meet new people, encounter new opportunities, get sick, try something and don't like it, or get lost; we may decide to take a completely different route, or a detour changes the route for us. Tina lost her job, which completely disrupted the path she was on. A short time later her mother became ill. She couldn't figure out what to do. But being without work gave Tina the time to be with her dying mother: "I was able to get to know my mother better, deepen my prayer, and receive support and help from others. I came to know a whole world of support which I never knew I had."

As a pilgrim, being called by God means trusting in God's companionship no matter what happens along the way. Callings become a response that requires that we discern the path with God's guidance. For instance, I have always had a strong calling to be a teacher (something like the acorn), but I never sensed that God was calling me to one particular place to teach—in fact, when choosing between offers at two good schools, I wanted God to send me some kind of message about which offer to accept. Wouldn't that make it easier if God did the choosing? But over time, I had the sense that God would be happy if I taught at either place. The choice was up to me; the deeper calling was to live out my calling to teach in whichever place I chose.

"You found it! You finally found it!"

Has God ever surprised you? "Aha!" experiences can reveal a direction or purpose that we might not have seen or understood, even though it was right in front of us. From the time he was a child, Ken had always enjoyed working with wood. While teaching high school wood shop, he decided to take a class in whittling. "It was an evening class, and all we had to do was cut little notches on a piece of wood the first night. I remember coming home and sitting there at the table cutting these

8

notches on the wood just trying to get them all even and getting used to using a knife and a piece of wood and doing it properly. And I was so excited. It was like my spirit was jumping inside. You found it! You finally found it! This is what you are to do. But at the time I figured this would be just like when I tried to learn to play guitar or play tennis. It would last a few months and then die off. But this never died. It just kept growing and growing."

Ken describes what many people discover when they identify an ability or develop a passion. They are awakened to a gift, and they fall in love in a way that never leaves them. Regardless of whether that gift becomes paid employment, many people find that callings are rooted in something they are given to do and love doing for others.

Each of these images—acorn, pilgrimage, and surprising discovery—is a key way to experience God's call. The images tell us that vocation is something we make with God, who can be known and named as planner, walking companion, and gift giver. In this sense our experiences of God and vocation are better understood on a continuum from the highly detailed to the less precise, with everything in between.

This proved true during the summer after my senior year of high school when I volunteered in a six-week service program. I had a sense that God was guiding me to a life of service to the sick or the hand-icapped, but I wanted to experience it before I set off to make it my career. I was disappointed when I was not assigned to the hospital I wanted and ended up in Georgia teaching in a Bible camp for grade-school children. I was sure this was not my calling, since I had no gift for teaching children. For the first few weeks, things did not go well for the leader or for me—no doubt I was grumbling about my unfair situation. The leader finally told me not to come back to the camp, but to go and visit the sick if that's what I wanted to do. With that, the team left me alone to figure it out. I had a list of parishioners, but very little desire to go meet strangers by myself in a community I'd never been part of. The list included Marv, a paraplegic in the county nursing home, a really smelly place. So, in-stead of visiting the sick, I hung around and slept most of the day.

During one afternoon nap I had a dream in which my name was shouted at me: "Kathleen." Startled, I woke up. I mean I really woke up, not just from the nap, but from my laziness. I heard God *shouting* at me. I had just one week left. I grabbed the list and visited everyone in the parish, including Marv. When I went to college the following autumn, I wrote "Kathleen" on the registration form rather than "Kathy," the name I had been called as a child.

Some people experience callings as a choice they make, while others sense that they have no choice but are born into their vocation or given gifts they must use. When you hear God's call in your life and in the lives of those around you, remember to affirm that God has many ways, not just one way. Furthermore, if you think your life includes many calls at different times, you may begin to experience vocation in a more dynamic and plural way.

CHAPTER 2

Called **to** Be Followers of Christ

"Then Jesus called his disciples to him."
(Matthew 15:32)

As a youth, I had a strong sense of God's call to the service program I entered after high school. I also heard a calling to teach as a young person, and as an adult I experienced a calling to be married. Much of the way we talk about vocation is about being called to—to someone, to somewhere, or to something. If Christians have a sense of vocation, it is usually tied to the big decisions of our lives: the choice of a school, a job, a mate, a place to live. I know that when I face big decisions, I would rather it be like entering a search into Google Maps and following the directions. I want something that confirms that my choices are on the right path, since committing to this place or this person means I have said no to other places or people.

What are you called to? How have you been called to follow Christ? What is unique about the callings in your life? Do you experience many callings in your life? If so, how do they connect to each other?

"...then come, follow me." (Mark 10:21)

The word "disciple" means "one who follows." In the time of Jesus it often referred to one who followed the teaching of a great teacher. Jesus was not the only teacher with disciples, but he differed from other teachers and their followers. Many people would follow the teachings of one teacher for a time, but then switch and follow another teacher—like following a talk-radio show for several years, growing tired of the message, and searching the dial for a new personality. But Jesus was different in at least two major ways. First, he called his disciples to follow him rather than the disciples choosing to follow him. To keep with my analogy, the radio host would select the listeners; the listeners would not select the host. Second, his "way" was radical, requiring disciples to change their heart and mind, to give up loyalty to job, family, friends, and nation in order to embrace Jesus's way of life—which included breaking religious laws, eating with sinners, and facing persecution. As disciples of Jesus today, we are called in the following ways: to be a follower, a worshiper, a witness, a neighbor, a forgiver, a prophet, and a steward.

What do you think it means to be a follower of Christ? After all, even in the Gospel accounts not everyone who is invited to follow becomes a follower. At the outset of Mark's Gospel, for example, "the whole crowd gathered around him" (Mark 2:13) and "a great multitude from Galilee followed him" (3:7), but near the end of the Gospel, he had been abandoned even by his disciples. Some who want to follow hear what they must do and decline the offer. A man comes and kneels before Jesus asking what he must do to inherit eternal life, but Jesus's response—sell everything, give it to the poor, "then come, follow me"—is rejected. The man was "shocked and went away grieving," for he could not give up his possessions, his way of life, to follow Jesus (10:21–22).

Some who hear and accept the message do follow. They recognize who Jesus is and address him as "Lord," a term related to homage and to worship. In Matthew's Gospel, the leader of the synagogue seeks Jesus's help in restoring the life of his daughter, and when he addresses Jesus, he falls on his knees (Matt. 9:18), a gesture reminiscent of the Magi, who "knelt down and paid him homage" (2:11). To be a follower, then, is *to be a worshiper*, one whose heart is filled with adoration and love for the source of life, the One on whom we depend.

In what ways have you responded to Jesus as a worshiper? Sherice, for example, loves to sing, both at work and at church. Working in a large corporation in the publishing and marketing division, she has some tough days, but singing helps keep her focused on God's presence in her midst. "I can sometimes sing because I am upset and I do need to calm down. If I'm having a difficult day on the job I may need to just walk out and take some time alone, and sing, 'I give myself away.'" Our worship is the recognition of the goodness and power of divine blessing in our lives—we rejoice, falling on our knees and singing God's praises. "I give glory to God," Sherice says, whether singing on the job or in the church choir.

As disciples, we are each called *to witness* to what God has done for us. We see models of witness in many of the New Testament healing stories, where the person whose life is changed wants to go and tell everyone—to witness to what God has done for him or her. For example, two blind men recognize who Jesus is and he heals their sight, but they can't seem to heed his words not to tell everyone: "They went away and spread the news about him throughout that district" (Matt. 9:31). To be a witness is to be called to tell the truth about what God is doing in your life. You are a witness whenever the story you tell about your life reflects the many ways God has called, nurtured, converted, or healed you. Anna, who works at a large state university, wears a cross that offers students an open invitation to talk to her about their religious questions and the spiritual life. "I don't roam the halls telling students to follow Jesus. That wouldn't be right here," she says. "I live my life as an example, and when they come and seek me out, I'm ready to share my faith with them. And my cross is a sign that my faith is in Jesus."

The call to be a neighbor, like the other aspects of discipleship, reaches far back into the Hebrew Scriptures, where laws were formed about how neighbors were to treat one another. The term "neighbor" refers to one who dwells nearby, or lives alongside, and ancient laws protected people from harming one another and their property. They also encouraged care beyond one's family and tribe. How are you called to be a neighbor to those around you?

When I was a graduate student, I took a year from full-time work to write my dissertation. I had a small study that overlooked my garden, and it was quiet and peaceful. It was a perfect place to write each day with no interruptions. From my window I could see the houses across the street. Shortly after I started on my thesis, a neighbor across the street was diagnosed with esophageal cancer, and she quickly declined. Soon she was receiving hospice care at home. The staff situated her medical bed in the front window of her house. Now my window looked across the street at her window: I was literally looking at a dying woman each day. Here I was writing a dissertation on prayer and the moral life, from which I did not want to be interrupted, and my neighbor was dying, literally, in front of my eyes!

I had to do something—I couldn't write a word, and yet I couldn't give up my entire day to be with her. I finally walked over and asked her mother, "What can I do? I live across the street, and I don't know Tammy very well, but I'm home each day and I could help if you need me." The mother was overjoyed and said, "Could you open the door every morning for the hospice worker so I don't have to come first thing?" That was it—that was all she asked of me.

In the New Testament Jesus turns the neighbor law on its head, expanding the definition of neighbor beyond kin and friend to include the poor, the outcast, and those we despise, when he proclaims, "Love your enemies and pray for those who persecute you" (Matt.

5:44). Such neighbor relations are never easy, whether they involve those next door or those on the other side of the globe, because we tend to judge our neighbor unfairly and hate those who harm us, seeking vengeance and attacking with words and weapons.

Because we fail to heed the call to neighbor love, Jesus also calls disciples *to be forgivers.* To learn to forgive those who harm us and to seek forgiveness when we harm others is the radical edge of Christian discipleship. I think it is the hardest thing to learn, probably harder than love. But there is no such thing as neighbor love without forgiveness. Forgiving one another, for Jesus, is tied directly to our relationship with God: "For if you forgive others their trespasses, your heavenly Father will also forgive you; but if you do not forgive others, neither will your Father forgive your trespasses" (Matt. 6:14–15). Karen struggled to forgive Keith, her husband, when he was unfaithful and left the family. "I knew God wanted me to forgive Keith, but I just couldn't after what he did to me and the kids," Karen said. "But eventually I found a way to stop hating him and realized God didn't want me to be angry the rest of my life."

Because we are such poor neighbors at times, we are also called *to be prophets*—to declare what is wrong with our neighborhoods and call our neighbors back to right relationship through justice and mercy. Each of us is called at times to be prophetic about injustices we encounter, to work toward changing the conditions that crush our neighbors, including our enemies. To be a prophet is to be unpopular because it requires us to tell truths, even to those we love. Adrián knew there was a problem at his company in the business office. "I just had this inkling that something was wrong with the books, but I did not want to be a whistleblower. If I was wrong, my colleagues would hate me for pointing the finger at them, and if I was right, I may end up in a courtroom. Either way, I could lose my job, which I could not afford. In the end, I did the easiest thing: told my boss and asked him not to get me involved. It's the only time I really had to be a prophet and I hated it." When have there been times when you felt called to be prophetic? Did you embrace the call readily or cringe at the prospect?

To be a follower also means *to be a steward*, which means "one who cares for the household." Biblically, stewardship refers to the household of God's creation and to the goods of the home, such as food, shelter, animals, and the land. The good steward, as Jesus points out, is wise and prudent in caring for the goods of the master (Matt. 24:45–51). To be a steward is to heed God's call to care for all creation, accepting it as a gift, not as something we own and control. Paul goes further. He writes that Christians are to be "servants of Christ and stewards of God's mysteries" (1 Cor. 4:1). We are to be stewards of God's stories as well.

Dorothy describes the moment she realized she was called to be a steward of creation. After a long day spent cleaning up an abandoned mine site in the Cascade Mountains (where a copper mining town has been turned into a retreat center), Dorothy and a group of women were gazing at a meteor shower shooting across the sky. She suddenly understood that she was called to join with God and this community of disciples in renewing the face of the earth:

> At some point I became aware of a startling paradox. I was on top of a massive, toxic scar on the face of the earth. And I was also surrounded by a beauty beyond human imagining. A few decades before, human beings had wrecked the land beneath us; they had made money, and I had benefited too as a place of retreat became available to me. But the earth had paid a price. Fish could no longer survive in the river below, and deer could not drink of it. Even so, it was plain God still loved this land and these creatures, including us, including me. God was somehow about the work of renewing and re-

claiming it all. With the psalmist, I rejoiced: "Praise the Lord, across the heavens, from the heights!" Blessed be this strong darkness, these streaming lights, this silence, this promise of God to make all things new.

How have you been called as follower, worshiper, witness, neighbor, forgiver, prophet, and steward? How do you share this calling with other Christians?

We have a common, shared calling as Christians. Discipleship is our most foundational and fundamental identity and vocation—we are called *together* to be a community of disciples. In fact, in the New Testament the term "disciple" is rarely used in the singular; it appears over two hundred times in the plural—"disciples." I am not a disciple alone as an individual, but rather I belong to a community of disciples because I share in the "one body and one Spirit ... called to the one hope of [our] calling, one Lord, one faith, one baptism, one God ... of all" (Eph. 4:4–6).

"With God as the center of my life, I know whose I am and can begin to discover who I am."

Is discipleship one calling or seven callings? If it is one calling, how do you live out different aspects of discipleship in your one life? If it is seven callings, how do you manage to do so much? Most people experience a multiplicity of callings:

- to relationships (e.g., spouse, parent, daughter, friend)
- to specific roles (e.g., coworker, teacher, volunteer, boss)
- to ways of being (e.g., loyal, encouraging, compassionate)
- to particular gifts or abilities (e.g., connector, thinker, provider, problem solver, blood donor)

Many people find great joy in living out multiple callings in different contexts, experiencing callings in midlife, at retirement, and in their elder years.

But there are challenges to being faithful in multiple callings. When your callings include multiple relationships and roles in varying contexts, your life is marked by responsibility, duty, and care for others. Young parents report the trials of switching gears from work to home and having too many tasks and responsibilities in one day. Some desire more Sabbath time, which is not always possible. Holding on to a job sometimes means you can't slow down. Exhaustion is another factor. "I put energy and time in so many places that I run out of gas," says Peter. He has to perform "triage" with his different callings. "I have to decide quickly what needs my attention and forget about everything else. I do pray to God to give me an answer, but I don't always get one. It's important to me, though, to keep in contact with God."

A deeper challenge is searching for "who I am" across these many callings. Do I have one calling in many roles, or do I have many callings each in a different role? Angela stopped working as a full-time interior designer when she had children. She loved her work and missed the creative parts of it, and found that staying home with children was tedious at times and a real struggle. One day, she looked at her daughter and decided it was time to do something different. They headed to the art store and bought supplies. Angela realized from that day on that "I can still be a creative person, I can be who I am at my core, and still be a parent. There is nothing more creative than being a parent." She found a way to live out this one calling in her many roles.

Magazines, websites, and TV shows offer advice on how to achieve a greater sense of balance in our lives in these many roles. Jack Fortin says that a balanced life is a myth, since it points to our desire to control our lives. He says that the alternative is a "centered life," faithful to God in each moment. "The perfect example of the faithful life is Jesus Christ. Jesus often worked long hours despite the objections of his disciples, and at other times he withdrew from people and tended to his own needs for rest, reflection, and prayer.... A life centered in the triune God gives identity and a place to stand in a chaotic and compartmentalized world. The Creator God is present in all I do. Christ is the example and provides the means for how I am to live and love in God's world. The Holy Spirit is the voice within me that guides the way I live. With God as the center of my life, I know *whose* I am and can begin to discover *who* I am."

The experience of multiple callings may be challenging at times, pulling us this way and that way. But, as many discover, God's call can be found in each part of your life, which eventually gives direction, meaning, and purpose to the whole of your life.

*"The life I am living is not the same
as the life that wants to live in me."*

Psychologist and theologian John Neafsey describes vocation as a calling to listen and discover our "true self." God is calling us to truth, authenticity, and integrity. "God's call is directed . . . to the inner voice, the Voice of God," he writes. Neafsey says that God's voice is within each of us as a source of divine wisdom, "mysteriously both beyond and within ourselves." He writes, "God *uses* the inclinations of our true self, the promptings of conscience, to help guide and call us through decisions big and small toward the goal or purpose for which we were created."

The goal of vocation, then, is to find and live out of God's truth, a truth that takes on particularity in your life—the truth of who you are and how you live. You live out the truth of your life by following the path of discipleship shared with other Christians, but it will always be your unique story and life.

Parker Palmer, the Quaker educator and writer, articulated his struggle to give up the "false self" and to find his "true self." As a community organizer and teacher, Palmer was living a life according to others' expectations of what they wanted him to do; he was doing what he could to bring himself fame. However, neither stroking his ego nor pleasing others gave him much satisfaction; in fact, both made him pretty miserable. It felt too false, too untrue to what his life called him to, which was a greater authenticity about who he was as a person. The path of vocation entails shedding the false self that is often constructed by destructive messages, unrealistic hopes, or others' expectations. As Palmer states, "Before I can tell my life what I want to do with it, I must listen to my life telling me who I am. The life I am living is not the same as the life that wants to live in me." When he discovered the "true self" calling out to him, he followed that path and was able to work and be in relationship in a more congruent way. Palmer was not living a bad life, one of sin and debauchery. He was just not true to his real calling.

But the false self, in the Christian story, also refers to the way our lives become mired in sin. God calls us away from our selfishness and self-destructive ways not only because they hurt others, but also because they destroy the person God calls us to be. Many of us can resonate with Paul's claim that "I do not understand my own actions. For I do not do what I want, but I do the very thing I hate" (Rom. 7:15). The false self seeks its own good, making "me" important. The call of discipleship is to give up this self, to lose our life in loving service.

You experience the calling of the true self when there is something you know you cannot *not* do. It is as if you have no choice because the power to do something is so strong that if you denied it, you would not be true to God or yourself. Jane was pursuing a career as an actress, first in Chicago at Second City and then in Hollywood. She was good and getting better. But she had a second love and desire: ministry with women, particularly offering spiritual direction and retreats. Much of her young adult life found her moving back and forth between the two—when she was not acting, she'd find some ministry to do, and when not doing ministry, she'd be acting. But it was exhausting and there was something not quite right—she wanted a clearer sense of which path to pursue. She shared her dilemma with a person she met at a conference, who asked her, "Jane, imagine that you can only do one thing. If you could only act and never do ministry, how would that feel? Or, you can only do ministry and never act again, how does that seem?" In an instant she knew the answer. "Acting was something I could not do, but ministry was something I could not *not* do."

As a disciple, you are called to be a witness to what God has done in your life, but God also calls you to give your life as a witness to the truth about who you are. This is a long process, one that most of us have to live into and discover over time. You face the challenge of integrating what you do (work and service) with how you live (married or single), with who you are and are becoming. Much of adult life, particularly the middle years, pushes toward a greater connection between our multiple callings. It is finding what Paul calls "our way of life" for which God "made us" (Eph. 2:10).

CHAPTER 3

Called *as* We Are

God calls you in the particularities of your life.

Do you define yourself by your work or roles? We each long to be *someone*, not just someone doing something. All people want to be valued for who they are, not just for what they do. For most, it is a lifelong journey to discover who they are.

Have you experienced the call to be who you are as a bit of a mystery? Start with where you are. The preposition "as" relates to the particularities of your life, the conditions of your existence that are unique to you. God calls you *as* the person you are in the particularities of your life. You can only live out your vocation *as* the person you are; I can only become the person I am called to be in the context of my life. Does your name reflect something unique about who you are? What is specific to your family, schooling, work, and life commitments? How have you experienced God's callings as a youth or young adult, or in retirement or the elder years? Context shapes our callings.

———

"I've called you by name; you are mine" (Isaiah 43:1)

We each have unique and particular callings. God calls each of us *by name*. In the early church, a catechumen preparing for baptism received a new name, marking his or her new identity as a Christian. Several characters in the Bible took new names, marking a radical conversion: Abraham was Abram, Peter was Simon, and Paul was Saul. In the early centuries of the church, it became common at baptism to name a child after a holy person, a martyr or saint, to confer the child's identity and the meaning of the holy person's life on the child. Taking a new name became common at confirmation (usually an additional name); at marriage in Western countries a woman changed her name to the husband's family name.

The phenomenon is true in other religions. Jews

who live in the diaspora (outside Israel) can have both a secular and a Hebrew name connoting their religious identity. When a person becomes a Buddhist, the person can be given a new "Dharma name" that refers to the person's "taking refuge" in the Buddha. Several famous Muslims took new names in their conversion to Islam, such as the boxer Cassius Clay, who became Muhammad Ali.

My name, then, expresses something about who I am and whose I am. I heard my baptismal name called to me in a dream. When I went to college and enrolled as "Kathleen," I was taking back my original baptismal name. I didn't need God to give me a list of things to do in that dream; I needed to hear my name to know my calling—"Go and live the calling you have been given. Get up and serve others!" God was saying to me. My name is important to me because of this story, and even to this day when I hear my name called by another, I sense a deep resonance that God calls all of me to serve.

God's call to you is not a generic calling, but is specific to your time in life and place in the history of the world. My story is *as* particular *as* is your story. I was born a female and raised in Iowa, in the middle-to-late half of the twentieth century, to white, Irish immigrants who farmed the land; my parents, one Irish Catholic and the other Irish Protestant, worked in middle-class jobs;

I attended Catholic schools through college, then graduate school, and currently I teach ministry and practical theology in a Catholic university in Minnesota. This is my life—it is not yours and not my sisters', though they share a great deal of it.

Vocation is God's call to your life's particularities as you know them, that which is a given in your life (gender, family, ethnicity, time in history) and what you can make of it (education, opportunities, relationships). Even your understandings of faith, vocation, and God arise from these contexts. Theologian Edward Hahnenberg discovered "the mystery that is my vocation in the mystery that is me." You have been given this life, and you have to discover God's call *as* you are.

Culture determines a great deal about your life. Being a white, middle-class woman from Iowa is quite different from being an African-American male from South Miami. Theologically, God creates each of us, regardless of our context, to be children of God, but we can only live out our callings within our time and place. What does vocation look like from the particularities of your life? What difference does it make if you are an immigrant from Haiti or England? If you are wealthy or poor? Male or female?

*"It is not about the doing which a human does;
it is about the doing which a human is."*

It is not uncommon to think that vocation pertains to the major decisions in young adult life, and that once we get the big questions settled the issue of vocation is over. Certainly decisions about work, marriage or single life, and where to make a home are major life callings, but it does a disservice to both young adults and everyone else to isolate vocation in one period of our life span. Vocation is not reserved for a select group of people (college students or ordained ministers), a particular lifestyle (marriage), or certain types of work (service-related jobs). Vocation is about the whole of your life, your whole life long. How was God calling you as an infant or child? And now, how might God's call relate to your development *as* youth, young adult, adult, and older adult?

Joyce Ann Mercer, writing on vocation and teens, says that "God calls youth *as* the young people they are. Christian youth have life-purposes that exist within the purposes of God not in spite of their young age, but because of it." We tend to treat youth and young adulthood as a time to get ready for adulthood—a "not yet" vocation rather than an "already" vocation in the here and now. And when people retire from full-time work, they may think their vocation is over. To rephrase Mercer, God calls you not in spite of your age, but *as* the age you are.

You develop in two ways. First, you become a person, with a sense of who you are, through relationships with others; through the in-between-ness of relationship, you construct yourself. According to psychologist Robert Kegan, meaning making is the central way in which you form a sense of self, identity, and purpose. Humans make meaning by organizing their perceptions, experiences, feelings, and thoughts and drawing out their significance. You "take in" the world around you and order it in such a way that you can "act on" it sensibly. From the time you are an infant, you are continually making yourself as you act and react through your relationships with others. Kegan says, "It is not about the doing which a human does; it is about the doing which a human is."

The second way you develop is obvious: you change over time. Human beings are not static, but continually in process. Physical, mental, and emotional capacities change, grow, and mature. You make transitions over the course of your development—when you learn to walk or lose your hearing—which require you to make new meaning from experience. Transitions disrupt your sense of self, your relationship to your body as well as the world around you. The old ways of thinking and acting will not work (being a child is not helpful in high school), and new situations must be integrated into who you are. Growing and changing is, as Kegan explains, like being born anew, "hatched out—but over and over again." At the crucial points of life-span transitions, the self you have constructed, he says, has to be "lost" in order for a new sense of self to emerge with new capacities. Human life, then, is more of an activity than a thing, "an ever progressive motion engaged in giving itself a new form." Life is motion, and the motion of development requires you to make meaning with each new life phase.

The ways in which you negotiate each transition in the life span can determine how well or how poorly you live into the new situation. If children are not given the opportunity to explore activities they enjoy doing or are good at, and are made to do activities they do not like and do not have talents for, they can become discouraged and disengaged, and develop low self-esteem. Children who are given such opportunities take up tasks with greater initiative and eagerness to learn and improve, and gain a stronger sense of who they are and what they are capable of. They may readily respond to a sense of calling from those around them.

Vocation, then, is Christian meaning-making. It refers to the ways we "take in," construct, reconstruct, critique, and identify what is significant in relationship to God and others. God's call comes to us from birth till the end of our days in multiple and varied ways. You experience God's call anew through particular developmental tasks that emerge in each part of the life span.

"For it was you who formed my inward parts; you knit me together in my mother's womb." (Psalm 139:13)

The psalmist proclaims that it is God who first gazes upon you as a child *in utero*, for "your eyes beheld my unformed substance" (Ps. 139:16), and actively creates and knits you together.

Because focusing your eyes takes several months to achieve, as a newborn you had to develop the capacity to see clearly. An essential feature of your growing vision of the world was your ability to see a parent's eyes gaze at you. Infants are called *to gaze and to behold* the world around them, beginning with the parents' faces.

If they behold faces of care, love, and concern, infants develop a sense that the world is safe, predictable, and good. Infants learn to trust that their needs will be met, and through the gazing back and forth, infants continue their calling to be connected to another beyond the womb.

As a child, what did you like to play? Is there any relationship between your play and what you do today? A central calling for children is to create, imagine, invent, and delight in. Children's play is akin to creation—they are continually creating worlds filled with laughter and delight as well as roles and rules. In play, children are fully immersed in the present. The wisdom figure in the book of Proverbs describes her activity at the creation of the world in terms of playing with God:

> When he marked out the foundations of the earth,
>   then I was beside him, like a little child;
> and I was daily his delight,
>   rejoicing before him always,
> rejoicing in his inhabited world
>   and delighting in the human race.
>
> (Prov. 8:29–31)

Childhood is also a time of trying on new roles, learning to be a student, taking responsibility in a family for chores or tasks, and playing at adult jobs. Through play and initiative, the child's world is meaningful with a sense of "what I am."

As a teen, did you try out different clothing styles, travel to new places, or shift around to different groups of friends and companions? Youth are called *to begin exploring identity*, developing a sense of "who I am." They do so by trying on "possible selves," different ways of being in their relationships with peers and adults. Interestingly, they develop the capacity for seeing what others see about them. As James W. Fowler notes, "I see you seeing me: I see the you I think you see." In this process, youth mirror back to others the person they want them to see, and through this mirroring try on potential ways of being in the world. What were the possible selves you tried on as a teen? How do you see this among teens today?

Forging an identity is particularly difficult in our culture because youth are saturated with "possible selves" formed by images and desires constructed by consumer culture. Many youth begin to awaken to a sense of injustice and unfairness in the world, compelling them to be prophetic voices for the marginalized, but they can also be lost in a sea of possibility about who they should become. To search and hear God's voice guiding them, youth need to imagine a possible self that has faith and integrity. They need to hear counternarratives of callings from people to live out a commitment to care for the earth, explore religious questions, overcome conflict and violence, and develop hearts of compassion.

Young adulthood is a time "to ask big questions and discover worthy dreams," according to Sharon Daloz Parks. One's twenties now constitute a distinctive period in the life span. Regardless of the path—college, work, the military, or volunteer service—young adulthood is a time to search, discover, and reframe the identity forged in youth. To make meaning, young adults reflect upon the values they have inherited from family and culture and begin to raise critical questions. Young adults are searching for meaning by "participating in an ongoing dialogue toward truth," according to Parks, so that they can "set their heart" toward a purposeful life. Their task is to find a place in society in which they discover answers to the big questions of purpose, vocation, and belonging: "Where, why, and with whom will I dwell, love, and work?" How did you answer, or are you answering, the questions of young adult vocation?

"Keep paying attention."

Adulthood marks a major portion of the life span in which we experience callings *to love and work.* Many adults make lasting and binding commitments to marriage and childbearing, and pursue employment that defines much of their waking hours. Many people want to seek love and work that are productive, creative, and purposeful for the good of society. For many, adulthood is marked by a sense of agency, power, and participation. But what happens in adulthood when we face disappointments in opportunities not realized and dreams not pursued?

Adults must grapple with the growing gaps between their desires and dreams and the realities they face. By midlife, many adults have worked for several years, and begin to question what they are doing and why. "Is this it? Is this all there is to my life? Am I on the right track? Should I stay doing what I am doing or should I do something else?" Disillusionment at work and at home, the struggle of raising children, facing a failed marriage, meeting the constraints of the body— these factors often accompany the realization that life is half over.

Diane always wanted to be a teacher and in fact taught in colleges and universities for twenty years. "For almost all of those years, the way had not been clear. I could only find work teaching for a semester or a year. Because of my other callings, as a wife and mother, I was not in a position to look for a job in another city. By the time I got to my early forties, I knew that I did not want to continue working hard for little money and no job security. Moreover, I wanted a professional place of belonging. I discerned that it was time to explore other ways to respond to my vocation as an educator."

Through midlife disillusionment, adults are invited to explore their callings once more. What is the meaning of your many callings? How can you respond with greater integrity and serve others through your love and work? Oftentimes the struggle to answer these questions reawakens a sense of purpose and meaning.

Diane discovered that she could serve as an educational consultant, but she missed teaching in the classroom. One night she wrestled with God in prayer. "How can I want to teach so much and yet have such a difficult time finding a permanent position?" But then, Diane says, "I heard a response: 'Keep paying attention.' And I did. I began writing and then I saw: paying attention was the foundation of my training and my concern for others, inviting them to pay greater attention to the relationships in their lives." What do you need to keep paying attention to?

Adulthood hinges on two major transitions: the young adult search for life commitments, and the retirement phase when some commitments, usually full-time work, come to an end. Retirement is a major if not central vocational moment in people's lives, as great as, if not greater than, the young adult years. But the category of "retirement" no longer fits our situation today. It became a cultural pattern and norm after World War II, with the advent of Social Security, when the life span was much shorter and people did not live long after retiring from work. Today, things are much different in North America, as the average life span lengthens. We are not going to be elderly longer; we are going to be adults longer. What will, or does, calling mean in the later years of your life?

———

"And I shall dwell in the house of the LORD
my whole life long." (Psalm 23:6)

"I think since I've retired, I've had to look at what I'm good at and what I'm going to do with the rest of my life. I think I have gifts and I think I'm here to serve. I've been given a lot. I'm reasonably smart and can put things together. What is next for me?" asks Peg, a recently retired schoolteacher.

The calling in later adulthood is *to step back and step back in.* But the transition can be difficult, even bewildering, because it requires discernment about what to do with one's life. Many love their work, having forged a strong identity in their roles, finding meaning and purpose in working with others, and struggle to imagine what kind of life to make beyond full-time work. Peg says, "I went from this clearly defined role in my life: a teacher. I think we're a society of doers and we define who we are by what we do and I wasn't doing anything. I wasn't working. I wasn't volunteering. Health was an issue, so I had some limitations. It was sort of an excuse for why I hadn't figured it out. It was really hard to put together what was going to come next. I never expected the struggle."

Even for those who have not enjoyed their job and find the prospect of not working a relief, questions from young adulthood return: Where will I live? Whom will I love? How will I serve? What will I do? Many people in late adulthood want to make a contribution to their community. Some continue to do work in areas related to their professions, and others take on new work or activities. Many enthusiastically embrace the calling to be a grandparent, and some find themselves as caregivers for parents, spouses, friends, and sometimes children and grandchildren. Peg has found new meaning in simple acts of caring for her neighbors and friends. "When I look at what I've done in the last year, I've taken care of people in a variety of ways. I have some friends with some health concerns, and I've been available in a way that I never could be when I was teaching."

God's callings are not complete; they continue in older adulthood. The elder years come with a sense of ambiguity and uncertainty as the body changes, chronic illnesses persist, and people find they need to accept the care of others. Elders also experience many relationship losses, such as the deaths of spouses, friends, and family members, and they lose important roles as homemaker, cook, gardener, and provider. They may face the decision to find new living arrangements. Many live with a fear of the unknown.

The elder years are also marked by joy for those who find purpose and meaning in their changing situations. Relationships can take on new meaning, as some enjoy the wisdom they can share with others, remaining a loyal and committed friend to those undergoing transition and loss. The elder years, then, are marked by callings *to give and to let go*. In the midst of growing old,

God's call to the elder is to trust, as the psalmist proclaims, that

[God's] steadfast love endures forever,
and his faithfulness to all generations.

(Ps. 100:5)

God's callings are multiple and varied in your life,
emerging in different ways, given your age and the developmental tasks you face. Vocation is not static or lin-
ear, but dynamic, sometimes fluid and at other times
more stable. It is complex and multifaceted and is not
determined once and for all in your life. Called by name,
you can seek a "centered life," a truth about who you
are in the very particularities of your life. Across the
life span, God calls us as infants to gaze and behold, as
children to play, as youth to begin exploring identity,
as young adults to ask big questions and dream big
dreams, as adults to love and work, in later stages of
adulthood to step back and then step back in, and in
elder years to give and to let go. Where are you right
now along the path of life?

CHAPTER 4

Called *from* People, Places, or Situations

"Go from your country and your kindred and your father's house." (Genesis 12:1)

Have you ever had a calling *from* something, someone, or somewhere? A sense that God was calling you *from* but without a sense of where you might be going *to*?

Denise loved accounting but found she was being called *from* it. "When I was on the accounting team, it was like God wrote a job description for me. But later I felt God's call in a visceral way to get out of my work. My son was going through a hard time in high school and I was working long hours as president of my company, traveling overseas and building the business. I was out of town and had a dream and I heard a voice that said, 'Come home.' I prayed for the courage to answer that call and finally asked for a leave of absence from my job. My family needed me. God had a hand in that."

Being called *to* something, someone, or somewhere is often exciting and an adventure. But callings *from* somewhere, someone, or something can be bewildering and difficult. Several biblical narratives reveal the call *from*: Abraham is called *from* his homeland to a new place; Moses is called to lead the Israelites *from* slavery to the Promised Land, but it is a long way off; Naomi is called *from* the place where her husband and sons have died. The New Testament story of discipleship is also a *from* story: disciples are called *from* their jobs and homes to follow on the way. The way looks glorious at the outset, but it looks like it will end at Golgotha. Jesus is called *from* his ministry and community of friends to embrace the way of the cross.

To be called *from* entails moving away, an ending, before a new beginning is clear. This preposition captures the times of transition when you may have more clarity about the *from* than the *to*. It requires you to trust that moving away is the right path, a calling, even though you do not know the destination.

"The lifelong theme of finding and losing"

Many of life's transitions are exciting and mark a new start, but they are also painful and difficult. Do you ever wonder why we feel sad at a graduation or a wedding? We celebrate a young person's accomplishment at graduation, but the ceremony also marks an ending. Even when a young adult has secured work beyond high school or college, the unknowns of life loom ahead. Weddings are joyous, but they are also endings—the family as we've known it is changing. Another person is joining the clan; and not only does the new spouse become part of your extended family, but also the new spouse's family. For the couple, being single ends; a lifelong commitment begins, and neither person knows on the wedding day what life together will become.

Have you retired or are you thinking about it? Retirement from full- or part-time work is a significant life transition. We know what is ending—the job title, identity, the paycheck, the daily routine of going to work, and the relationships—which is far more certain for many people than what the next step will be. Many retired adults will admit that they could not see a clear direction until they left behind full-time work and

started into new forms of service, leisure, and meaningful work.

It took Bob years to retire. He loved his work as a
landscape architect and could not imagine what he was
going to do when he left the company. After years of
full-time work, he could not see how he would fill up
his day. He knew he did not want to golf all the time, nor
did he want to relocate to a sunnier climate. "But I knew
it was time to go," Bob said. "There was just something
about work that was ending. I still loved it but that love
was waning. I didn't have the same energy for it, and I
kept wondering if there was something more I was to
do with my life."

Bob's transition into retirement started with an ending. That's the first phase of life transitions: they begin
with an ending. Where there are endings, there are loss
and grief. Grief is a normal emotional response to any
type of loss, such as the loss of an object, a relationship,
a role, a function, or a community. The reason grieving
a loss is difficult is because we are creatures made for
relationship and we become deeply attached to that
which we love. A child who loves a doll or blanket will,
at some point, lose it or give it up, and for many children
the loss of a beloved object is the first significant loss
of an attachment. The psychologist Robert Kegan says
that as infants we have to begin the process of differen-

tiating ourselves from our parents, which "brings into being the lifelong theme of finding and losing."

We learn the rhythm of finding and losing again and again. The choice, of course, is not *not* to attach to people, places, or things. Rather, the life task we learn is how to attach to whom and what we love, relinquish the attachment when it is lost (which does not mean forgetting it), and reconstruct a meaningful life. It sounds easy, but we all know that the loss of an object, a relationship, a job, a marriage, an identity, or a community is painful; the death of a loved one draws us into some of the deepest grief we experience. There's a pilgrimage involved, a wandering aimlessly at times—the second phase of a life transition. The in-between time. Eventually the journey of grief enters a third phase— the challenge of reconstructing our lives and finding a new sense of purpose and meaning. God's callings are all along this pathway.

"My joy is gone, grief is upon me, my heart is sick."
(Jeremiah 8:18)

But what does vocation, God's call, have to do with transitions and grief?

Ultimately God calls you *from* your losses, but first God calls you to grieve. It seems that grieving is the only way to get *from* here to there. Grief is normal; what is abnormal is not to grieve. Through your grief you can encounter God's callings in several ways. First is to not deny the pain of your loss, but to undergo it. God calls you to enter into the emotions of grief—the numbness, emptiness, loneliness, isolation, fear, anxiety, guilt, shame, anger, sadness, despair. No wonder you don't want to grieve—these are painful human emotions you usually try to avoid. But denying your feelings means denying the way God made you. Emotions are a key way of being human, and God wants you to know and experience something through your emotions. If you deny the feelings, you deny the loss.

When Karen's husband left her after fifteen years of marriage and three children, she was outraged. She felt "called" to marry Keith and have children, and thought they had an ideal life together, except that he found someone else. "I was so jealous I tried to find out who she was and where she lived," Karen said. "And the next day, I'd try to forget that and cry all day, but by evening I was screaming at the kids. I couldn't even talk to Keith about an 'amicable divorce.' I thought there was no way I could live as a divorced person—I was married, for goodness' sake!"

The loss of a significant role or a relationship, especially a marriage, is tremendous. Karen felt anger, jealousy, rage, hurt, but also shame, guilt, and blame. As she said in one burst of emotion: "What could I have done wrong? How could he be such a jerk?" The emotions come like a roller coaster—one minute you are raging, another minute weeping. The tumult is actually quite normal in an initial loss. The role and relationship constitute a large part of who you are, and when they are gone, you are at a loss. The question "Who am I?" comes back. Karen was losing Keith, the dream of a future together, the family as she had known it, and the identity of being a married person.

Over half of the psalms are lament psalms, cries of agony, grief, and anger expressed to God. They are filled with human pain and brokenness:

How long, O LORD? Will you forget me forever?
How long will you hide your face from me?

How long must I bear pain in my soul,
and have sorrow in my heart all day long?

(Ps. 13:1–2)

To live and to love is to experience the emotions of loss and pain; to be in relationship with God means calling upon God with our full range of emotions.

Telling stories is essential to grief. You have to remember in order to let go. It seems counterintuitive since most people think that by forgetting the loss the pain will go away, but in fact, quite the opposite is true. Telling stories, creating memories, and recalling the meaning of the person, place, or thing actually help you to reconstruct your life. You step back in order to step forward. It is by placing the loss in the past that you can begin to look ahead, toward a different future. Of course, this never happens overnight. Grief doesn't follow a series of neat steps. The only way through is to keep telling your stories about the loss.

Grief also entails forgiving and possibly reconciling with another. Is there someone in relationship to this loss that you need to forgive—perhaps yourself or God? God's call is to forgive, even if reconciliation with another is not possible: we are called to forgive ourselves, to forgive another, and to receive another's forgiveness. Without forgiveness, memories turn to resentments, nagging arguments rage in your mind, and you find yourself rehearsing conversations over and over again. You are not free, but bound to your hurt and wounded heart. God calls you *from* this hurt, and promises to accompany you through the path of forgiveness. Like grief, forgiveness calls you to embrace the pain of being hurt, to make a firm decision to forgive, to reframe your image of the person who hurt you (the person is not the worst monster in the world), to release the hold the injury has on you, and to deepen a sense of yourself as one injured and free *from* the emotional pain.

Years ago Karen was called to marriage but now found she was being pulled *from* it and not by choice. Over time, God began to call her *from* her grief and sadness and to put the marriage in the past. "I knew it was over and I knew I had to move on and forgive Keith for what he did to me and the kids. If I didn't I was going to be angry and bitter the rest of my life, and I knew that is not what God wanted for me. So I made up my mind to forgive him and let the pain and anger go. I have still not reconciled with Keith, but I hope to be able to one day. I always loved him and I would like to be able to see him at family events and at least be friendly to him and his new wife." What Karen hopes for is reconciliation—the mutual forgiveness and acceptance between two parties—a further step beyond forgiveness.

*"Blessed be the LORD, who has not left you
this day without next-of-kin; and may his name
be renowned in Israel!" (Ruth 4:14)*

Another aspect of life transitions and grief is to reintegrate the loss into your life and to embrace life again. The point of grieving is not to forget what you lost, as if you could. The point is to move away *from* the strength the loss has in your heart, and to form new attachments. God is calling you to life, to continue creating your life in and through the divine purposes. God is calling you to hope that life can be meaningful again, that you can love, and give yourself to places, people, and things again. After a time of grief, gratitude can emerge, even from very painful losses. We are grateful for our lives and ready to respond to our callings again. God is calling us from our old attachments to love again.

The biblical story of Ruth and Naomi recounts a terrible ending, a commitment to the unknown, and faith in forging a new life. After leaving Israel because of famine, Naomi loses her husband and her two sons in the land of Moab. She tells both of her Moabite daughters-in-law to return to their families because she has nothing to give them; she is returning to her family in

Israel. "'Go back each of you to your mother's house. May the LORD deal kindly with you, as you have dealt with ... me....' Then she kissed them, and they wept aloud" (Ruth 1:9–10). But Ruth refuses and says,

"Where you go, I will go;
  where you lodge, I will lodge;
your people shall be my people,
  and your God my God." (Ruth 1:16)

She returns with Naomi to Bethlehem and, after a roundabout way, marries Boaz and gives birth to a son. The women of the town exclaim to Naomi, "Blessed be the LORD, who has not left you this day without next-of-kin; and may his name be renowned in Israel!" (Ruth 4:14). Naomi and Ruth share in the tragedy of famine as well as the death of their spouses, but they remain together and forge a new life in a new place.

Loss is part of life. To be a person of faith means to live into this mystery, not looking for simple answers, but finding God's presence and call in your grief. You reconstruct who you are and how you want to live by reentering your relationships and community. This is the way of our callings. And it takes time.

Bob finally retired from his full-time job, felt depressed for a few months, but slowly began reading, having coffee with friends, and looking for things to do. One of his friends asked him to help out at the senior center with a garden project. "Bob, I know you are not working anymore, but we could use your advice about what plants to put in." Bob was ready to quit working, but wanted to do something. After his initial consultation about the garden, he began going to the center once a week. He took up visiting with the residents, and the director eventually asked him to give a demonstration on tending indoor plants. Before long Bob was a regular speaker and teacher at the center and began getting the older adults who were gardeners outside and digging in the dirt. "I had no idea I could teach like this when I was working," Bob said. "But it is just right for me. I don't need to work, but I can use my skills and I can be with people and make a difference in their lives. Helping the older folks grow plants is the best job I've ever had!" A calling he could not see emerged *from* the transition, once he had made it.

"The Lord is near to the brokenhearted, and saves the crushed in spirit." (Psalm 34:18)

The call *from* someone, someplace, or something is a strange call. It may not seem to you that the word "vocation" fits these experiences. If we step back, we can see that the biblical tradition testifies to God's presence in each aspect of loss discussed above: God *understands* the pain, *listens* to our story and invites us to listen in return to God's story, *forgives* us our sins and graces us to do the same for others, and *regenerates* our lives. God is calling us at each step of the journey.

God is continually calling us to new life, *from* our old ways, *from* our losses, *from* what has ended, into new ways, relationships, and beginnings. But in times of transition and grief we may discover something else about God: that our understanding of God, our "God," has not been helpful. We can be angry at God, blame God, and lament that God does not deliver us from pain and sorrow. But God may be calling us not only *from* our grief but also *from* our narrow views of who God is and what God does in our lives. Perhaps God is not the source of our suffering, but our companion and fellow mourner. Perhaps God wants us to know that no matter how painful life is, God's steadfast love endures forever. The biblical tradition is clear that God is "near to the brokenhearted, and saves the crushed in spirit" (Ps. 34:18). How might God be inviting you into a deeper understanding of who God is in relationship to your losses?

CHAPTER 5

Called *for* Service and Work

⸺

*Vocation is self-giving service
for the sake of God's world.*

What are your callings *for*? Walter is an actor, comedian, and magician, and he has found that his calling is *for* laughter and healing. A person with cancer told him, "Thank you! You gave me two hours of being cancer free!" A couple told him, "Thank you! This is the first night we have laughed since our miscarriage." And a marriage counselor told him he recommended his show to a couple and it turned their marriage around. The couple discovered that if they can still laugh together, they can work out the issues in their relationship. The marriage was worth saving.

Vocation is deeply personal because it is other-focused. If you think it is all about "you" and your development, you have distorted what Christian calling is about. God's call is to you *for* love of neighbor and service *for* others. Jesus teaches, "'You shall love the Lord your God with all your heart, and with all your soul, and with all your mind.' This is the greatest and first commandment. And a second is like it: 'You shall love your neighbor as yourself'" (Matt. 22:37–39). In the Christian story, *diakonia*, meaning "service," constitutes the path of discipleship. The truth about who you are and what you are *for* is the service you are called to give *for* others, *for* God's world. Jesus gave his life *for* you, and discipleship entails giving it back. Vocation, then, is self-giving service in community for the sake of God's world.

How do you know what your callings are *for*? In what ways are you called to serve? For whom is your service to be given? Can your employed work be a form of service?

———

Three questions

When discerning what you can give your life *for*, Michael Himes suggests that you reflect on three questions: Is what you are doing a source of joy? Is it something that calls forth your gifts, engaging your abilities and talents, using them fully? Is this role or work of genuine service to others and to the wider society? Or to put it another way, Himes says, "Do you get a kick out of it? Are you any good at it? Does anyone want you to do it?" Walter's story highlights each of these. He loves doing comedy and theater; he is good enough to be employed as an artist; and clearly people find his work meaningful in their own lives. When you experience work as a calling, there is a synergy among these elements. When one or more of them is missing, you know something is not quite right.

"There's not much they could do to get me to quit."

What kind of joy have you experienced in your work and service? Joy is a deep and abiding sense of well-being, confidence, hope, and goodness. For Himes, "joy" is not feeling good about what you are doing; rather, it is an "interior conviction that what one is doing is good even if it does not make one happy or content." Both happiness and pleasure can arise from joy, but joy is something more. It is a quality of being, an emotion, a sense of abundance and goodness.

The joy of being called *for* some service is akin to the deep truth I spoke of earlier. Have you ever experienced joy when work was difficult and demanding? For example, a study of zookeepers revealed that though they are highly educated and work in jobs that are low paying and offer little advancement, and include "dirty work" (cleaning up feces), zookeepers are so eager to work in a zoo that they volunteer at first in order to secure a job. One person said, "There's not much they could do to get me to quit," and another commented, "Even if I wasn't getting paid I would still be here." Zookeepers have found that caring for animals gives them such meaning and purpose that they experience a deep joy beyond the hardships it presents to them. One of the great joys they cited was the birth of an animal. As one said, "The last [species of animal] that was conceived and born in captivity was over 100 years ago and we're getting ready to do it again. Who couldn't get excited?!"

"Now there are varieties of gifts, but the same Spirit."
(1 Corinthians 12:4)

Discerning a calling *for* some work or service often re-sides in answering Himes's second question: What are my gifts, talents, and abilities? Your abilities that allow you to do something that changes things *for* the better are rooted in the Christian idea of gifts, which comes mainly from the New Testament writings of Paul.

Paul distinguishes two kinds of gifts. The first kind is the universal gifts of faith, hope, and charity that Christians receive through baptism that enable them to embody Christ's call to loving relationship with God and neighbor. A second kind of gift is charisms, which are particular and unique to each person. The term "charism" derives from the Greek word for "grace," which is *charis*, meaning a gift from God that, through its use, brings delight, joy, love, gratitude, pleasure, and kindness. Paul emphasizes the total free gifting of di-vine grace in salvation, a gift not granted because of merit or reward, but because of God's sheer love for each of us: "For by grace you have been saved through faith, and this is not your own doing; it is a gift of God—not the result of works, so that no one may boast" (Eph.

2:8–9). Grace is God's powerful love in relationship, an enacted love, a love continually present and calling forth our response. God has given us gifts for each other.

The grace of God is not however simply an un-qualified "gift" that you possess, like an object. Rather, charisms are described by pastors Jane Patterson and John Lewis as "a quite specific donation of the power of God into the world to do God's will for a whole community through God's relationship with a human being. In fact, it would be misleading to say that a person 'has' a charism, since the instances of *charis* are always on the move, from God through one or more people for the benefit of others, and especially for the benefit of a community of people who are committed to living abundantly in right relationship with one another." The experience of calling is a process that involves at least three entities: God, the person called, and the neighbor whom God loves. Recognition of charisms is a matter of getting clear about how God most often and most powerfully uses you as a means of God's gracious will for others. The joyful experience of a charism is a small-scale instance of the explosive joy of eternal life ("the *charisma* of God is life eternal in Christ Jesus our Lord" [Rom. 6:23]).

Zookeepers reported that they knew their calling was unique, but they had to do it. Many felt they had been gifted with a capacity to work with animals. One said, "When it comes to working with elephants, either you have it or you don't." Another commented, "I naturally wanted to stay here because I had a gift. I was here two days and I knew this is what I was meant to do."

Paul writes that the Spirit's particular gifts express different services: "For as in one body we have many members, and not all the members have the same function, so we, who are many, are one body in Christ, and individually we are members one of another. We have gifts that differ according to the grace given to us" (Rom. 12:4–6). You are not exempt from charisms (1 Pet. 4:10), but you also do not receive all the gifts or only one charism. You are a unique combination of gifts (1 Cor. 7:7). Like the human genome, in which there is a basic shared structure, no two persons are alike. You, and your neighbor, are each empowered uniquely by the Spirit.

Does anyone want you to do it?

Do you ever have the sense that someone or some community needs the gifts you have to offer? Have you received the unique gift another has to offer? Who needs your gift and services? What can you do, *for* whom can you do it, and does anyone want you to do it?

According to Saint Paul, there is only one reason the Spirit gifts you: to build up the community. Paul believes that the Spirit gives the community a variety of gifts for the purpose of building the common good: "Now there are varieties of gifts, but the same Spirit; and there are varieties of services, but the same Lord; and there are varieties of activities, but it is the same God who activates all of them in everyone. To each is given the manifestation of the Spirit for the common good" (1 Cor. 12:4–7). Charisms are fundamentally gifts for service; they are your capacities that are expressed through your activities, actions, speech, and practices. They are not private, internal qualities, meant for self-improvement. The Spirit ensures that charisms are always present in the community, that gifts are distributed that, if discerned and responded to, will enable the community to flourish in its mission (1 Cor. 12:11). Charisms express diversity within the community, a diversity that recognizes that the health of the body of Christ and the fulfillment of the community's mission are dependent upon the flourishing of many gifts (1 Cor. 12:12–13).

It matters that the work and service you offer *for*

others matter in their lives. As one zookeeper noted, "The animals never chose to be here and it's our responsibility to come in and give them the care that they need and make sure that they're healthy and happy."

"*Find your own Calcutta.*"

Like a series of concentric circles, your callings *for* others are lived out in multiple contexts. The center circle is your primary relationships—the call to serve family and close companions. Allison's son contracted Lyme disease, which went undetected for years, and now he cannot work and has suffered neurological damage. In the second stage of her adult life, after the death of her husband, she cares for this adult son. Furthermore, her daughter has a severely handicapped child, and Allison helps her a few days each week. The call to serve, for many of us, stays close to home.

Yet Jesus warns against letting family become an idol and failing to serve those beyond the family who live alongside us—a colleague at the office, a clerk at the store, a widower at church—all neighbors in our local context. Jesus, of course, did not think this was enough either. For him, neighbor love and service meant giving ourselves to the stranger, the poor, and the enemy. This is the widest circle encompassing our life. The neighbor command reaches toward all those we do not know or work with on a daily basis.

For most of us, serving the poor does not mean moving to Calcutta when the poor and outcast are in our communities. It means, as Mother Teresa told a woman who wanted to join her community, "find your own Calcutta." Gayle, who grew up in poverty, knew that financial security was necessary, but eventually realized it could not be an end in itself. "The only thing I thought of when I was young was I needed money to be secure. I did not want to end up like my mother, who was a widow with no money for her family. So I worked as hard as I could to get my security, but it's not enough," said Gayle. "I'm now trying to start a nonprofit to help serve the poor. I know God is telling me to 'keep doing exactly what you are doing!'" Vocation connects your gifts to the well-being of others so that your community might thrive, even flourish. It's a true calling when it makes a difference for others.

"The very first demand that his [a carpenter's] religion makes upon him is that he should make good tables."

How many hours do you work, if you are employed? Americans work a lot. In fact, full-time employees work, on average, forty-seven hours per week, one whole day more than the norm of forty hours. There are many reasons we work long hours: jobs are more demanding with more expertise required; we are linked via technology at all times to our work; we want to gain more income, often to keep up in a consumer-driven culture; and nationally, the real cost of living is much higher than it was forty years ago, while real income has declined. This makes it sound like working more is a curse, when in fact for many, work is a deep joy, a source of personal and social meaning, and purpose. These two dynamics of work—its difficulty and its blessings—are ancient teachings from the book of Genesis.

One of the central images of God in the Bible is God as worker. Genesis opens with the story of God working to bring about the creation and resting on the seventh day (Gen. 2:2). Throughout the Hebrew Bible, God works *for* the redemption of the people and the authors use metaphors of work to describe God: household manager, craftsman, artisan, gardener, potter. These images are drawn from the everyday world of people who saw in their own work something intrinsic about who God is and how God is in relationship to them. Because God is a worker, God calls us to work, alongside and with God. Since we are made in the image of God, our work reflects and participates in God's work—to labor for what brings life, overturns injustice, and sustains communities.

Have you ever found work not joyful or meaningful? The Bible also attests to the fact that work can be hard and at times meaningless. Anyone who works every day, laboring for food, shelter, and well-being, knows that to till the earth requires backbreaking effort, to run a business requires intense concentration and judgment, to nurse a sick person demands diligence in understanding the body and patience to endure another's pain and suffering. Difficulties are as much a part of work as are joys and blessings.

In calling you *for* a life of service to the common good, God can call you to work and in your work. Jerry knew that he was good at math and science; it just came easily to him, like a gift. He knew he could use this ability in many different ways, but he decided to become an engineer when he realized how creative and challenging it was to solve problems through designing and making things that work for people. He had a sense that God had given him this ability, and he wanted to use it for something good. He got a job with a large engineering firm after graduating from a top school, and he worked steadily to support a family. But the company was bought out by a bigger one, and his division and job were eliminated. He was stunned and angry, and felt deeply betrayed by the company to which he had given so much over the years. He would have to find another job at another engineering firm, but it would not be the same; he had lost heart for the job. In his anger he vowed never to give so much to another company or job again.

Jerry's story sheds light on an important insight: God calls us to the work in the job, but perhaps not to the job. In other words, God may not necessarily have a job in mind for us, a particular position in a particular company or organization. Rather, God has given us the capacities to do good work, and we find and discern the places to get a job or volunteer. Because we can become overidentified with a job, and lose our perspective and calling, this distinction is helpful. Jane was struggling to keep her business and ministry going because of caring for her father-in-law, when she realized that her business and ministry were to care for him. Work can become an idol for many. We worship work because it is a source of our self-worth, it feeds our desire for more money and goods, and it asks us to sacrifice our family and friends.

The work that you do is inherently good when it aligns with God's purposes, when your work is a service given for the common good. You may experience a deep resonance between who you are and what you are able to do. Your competence and excellence in your work is a sign of God's work in you. In the 1930s, the British writer Dorothy Sayers said that the church misses the point when it tells the carpenter not to drink and be disorderly. Rather, she says, the church should be telling him that "the very first demand that his religion makes upon him is that he should make good tables." What use is such work, she asks, "if in the very center of his life and occupation he is insulting God with bad carpentry"?

Your gifts and abilities, then, call you to do certain work, but it is also what you do in and on the job that constitutes your vocation. Martin Luther, for example, emphasized that any kind of work can be a Christian vocation—there is no higher or better job than another, because it is in the work of baking or making shoes that you are called to love God and serve your neighbor. Likewise, the computer analyst, shop clerk, and accountant can respond to God's call in the work they do.

Work has always been a means of sustenance, a way to provide food, shelter, and well-being for ourselves and our families, but work is not an end in itself. It is a means to a greater good, a good that is in service to the larger community. When Jerry's job at the company fell apart, he had to take a long look at himself: What was he doing and why? He had climbed high in the corporate structure, but he knew he had lost his purpose along the way and that being a good engineer was less important than the bonuses, titles, and prestige he received. The loss of the job was a chance to reclaim his calling: God wanted him to be a good engineer in order to use his abilities for the good of others, but he lost that calling in the job. Could he find a job where his true calling and gifts could be used?

The professions are important "because they stand for, and in part actualize, the spirit of vocation."

One way that Western societies have linked work and vocation is through the professions. A professional, according to philosopher William Sullivan, is someone who professes a body of knowledge and engages in skillful, competent practice, on behalf of others, in the setting of colleagues, for the purposes of serving the common good. The promise professionals make is to use their knowledge and skill, not for their own gain, but for the good of those they serve. When you visit an accountant, you expect her to represent your best interests, to know the tax code and interpret it correctly, and to use her time efficiently. In other words, you would not trust an accountant who was out to make a lot of money for herself, who missed the deductions pertaining to your tax return, and who cut corners to get the job done quickly. The same applies to the social worker, the doctor, and the first-grade teacher. Their promise to us is that our well-being is first and foremost in their work.

The relationship of professionals to those they serve is constituted by a bond of loyalty and trust. In fact, without this bond the common good of our society would erode. Professionals make a covenant to use their expertise on your behalf, and you entrust professionals with your well-being, whether it is your taxes, your health, or your children. This reciprocity is the basis for what Sullivan calls "civic professionalism." Consider the backlash when professionals abuse their authority and responsibility: police officers who racially profile citizens, clergy and coaches who sexually abuse, lawyers who lie, and bankers who steal. In these cases individuals are not living up to the purposes and ethical standards of their profession.

Professions are important, as Sullivan notes, "because they stand for, and in part actualize, the spirit of vocation." We share a common calling with others in our profession—we profess together. Obviously professions in American society are not religious, and yet they are a way in which we, as Christians, can live out God's calling to work *for* others.

Because serving the needs of others is a shared responsibility, professions uphold a sense of duty and responsibility; at times they require sacrifice. But "sacrifice" is jarring and offensive to some people. It may sound like Jesus is saying "be a doormat." For those who have been harmed or abused, this can be painful language, an untruth about their lives. In fact, you may be called to stand against oppression. When Jesus asks you to give up your life, he is saying: Give your life for the sake of love.

Sacrifice is, first of all, an act of praise and thanksgiving, and is related to gift giving. In the context of vocation, giving your vocation for the sake of others is a sacrifice—I give this gift out of love. It costs me, but I give it. In the face of responsibility and hardship, you can give it freely. Jane, who followed her calling to ministry, realized that when Jesus said, "Do this in memory of me," he meant the "this" to be more than the breaking of the bread. "Jesus was saying, 'break yourself, sacrifice yourself, give of yourself,' because when we do this and suffer for others, we are doing what Jesus is doing for us. We are remembering Jesus. We are being Christ's followers."

CHAPTER 6

Called **through** Each Other

⁓

"One God and Father of all, who is above all and through all and in all." (Ephesians 4:6)

God works *through* others to call us. Who has God worked through to call you?

Mike was called by God through his colleague, Arthur. Actually he was called out. Mike had been working in his dream job as Arthur's radio producer. At the invitation of a friend, Mike was leading weekend retreats for his parish, and when he returned from one Arthur noticed a change in him. He asked Mike, "So, what's her name?" "I'm not sure what you mean," Mike responded. "I haven't seen you this excited in months ... did you meet her this weekend?" Arthur replied. Mike told Arthur it was not a woman, it was a weekend retreat.

After several weeks, Arthur knew something was different about Mike and asked him, "Why are you working here? Mike, if you could be anything, what would you be doing tomorrow?" After much soul-searching, several conversations with Arthur, and some restless nights, Mike admitted to Arthur that he liked leading retreats because he enjoyed hearing people's real stories and helping them find meaning in their lives. "Well, go do that!" Arthur said laughingly. "And get the hell outta here!"

Most people say that they first experience a sense of calling through another person. Family, friends, or mentors highly influence a person's choice in work. Some people enter the profession of their parents or siblings. The discernment of your gifts and capacities for service begins when others around you notice and call them forth. Certainly youth and young adults require adults who can help them try out their gifts in different contexts. Mike needed Arthur to help him recognize what he would love doing beyond his current job. At times these calls confirm what we already know; at other times they come as a surprise—when a mentor or teacher sees gifts in you that you did not see and invites you to test them out.

We are utterly dependent on each other to become who we are, to hear God's callings, and to respond.

The parent-infant relationship points to this reciprocity in the most poignant way. Because infants cannot live without basic care, they "call" the mother and father into parenthood to provide for their needs. At the same time, the parents "call" infants into being through gazing, naming, holding, feeding, and nurturing them. The calls are reciprocal and intertwined, and yet each responds in his or her own unique way. People closest to you are the most significant factors in the calls you follow and the choices you make. If you are struggling to figure out what God is calling you *to* or *for*, listen to God's call *through* the people around you.

"*The deeper calling was to explore the restlessness.*"

But people can fail you. They can give you poor advice or encourage you to follow their path. Parents, teachers, and friends do not always listen to the story you are living, and may not be listening to God for you. Rather, they may have some other purpose or their own desires or values that they want you to live out. They may think they know what is best for you, but they may not be an agent *through* which you can hear

God's calling. People can discourage or deny a calling that you may hear.

Unfortunately, families and teachers often do not support a young person's dream. When Laura was in college she majored in French. Both her father and her teachers recognized that she was excellent at French and encouraged her to pursue graduate education and become a college teacher. But something did not seem right. As she was discerning her choices, she asked her French professor how she could live a life in which her faith and work were integrated. Her professor responded, "I just compartmentalize my life. I completely separate my faith from my work life." But compartmentalizing her life was not appealing to Laura. "I had so much anxiety about whether it was the right path for me that I decided to take a year off before applying to doctoral programs. I went to France and volunteered for a year at L'Arche and in a homeless shelter. I let my love of French lead me there because I wanted to use these language skills on a practical level and I wanted to immerse myself in another culture. And yet the deeper calling was to explore the restlessness, to imagine what my life might be like if I didn't leap into academia like everyone was pressuring me to do."

Some people, despite misdirection in early adulthood, are at a later point rerouted and pursue a calling they intimated earlier. Camila had to learn to depend on God because she could not depend on her parents. She wanted to be a missionary, but her parents wanted her to go to the best university. She has been able to merge both of these paths, working in human resources and also with her husband, who directs a Christian nonprofit agency providing emergency relief. "God," she says, "is faithful to my calling, finding ways of living it out despite my parents' discouragement." There is nothing wrong with wanting financial security for your children, but it cannot come at the expense of their calling.

While others may fail you, you may also fail others if you do not heed God's call to be an agent of vocation. In Luke's account of Paul's conversion, Paul is blinded for three days, trapped in his own tomb of darkness, and it is *through* a man named Ananias that Paul comes to see the light of Christ. Ananias receives a call he is not eager to follow. God asks him to go to Saul, a man who is murdering members of his community (Christians), and to heal him of his blindness. God assures Ananias that he has a purpose for Paul—"for he is an instrument whom I have chosen to bring my name before Gentiles and kings and before the people of Israel" (Acts 9:15). Ananias has to trust God and follow the call to visit and heal a person he hates and does not trust. Yet he is God's agent to call Paul away from his hatred. Both men are called to discover God's callings *through* the other.

―――――――

"Who comes into a person's life may be the single greatest factor of influence to what that life becomes."

You are God's agent of vocation. If your call is to be *for* others, then you must become a person *through* whom God's call is heard and heeded. For the community to hear God's calling, you must realize that, like Ananias, God is calling others *through* you. Robert Kegan notes that "who comes into a person's life may be the single greatest factor of influence to what that life becomes." When you have "come into" another's life, you have re-ceived your highest calling! Do you recognize the other's gifts? Offer opportunities for her growth? Listen when he is discerning his way? Guide her when she is lost? How have you as family member, friend, colleague, or mentor been an agent for others?

Callings begin in family. Jeff remembers his dad, who loved being a physician, urging him to "do something with your life that you love!" When parents are passionate about what young people are doing, they support and nurture their search and discovery of their callings.

Those who call include friends, colleagues, and supervisors who tell you the truth about yourself. When Lawrence was in college, he switched majors often. He thought he should go out and change the world, so he studied medicine, and then economics. Each time he switched majors he would ask his friends what they thought, and each time they replied, "No! That's not you."

We are also called through those we serve. Service is not a one-way encounter, a kind of paternalism or control over another. Through service we receive the gift of another person, a gift that can call us out. Janet, a college student, works as a nurse's assistant on a memory care unit. She has learned to love the people, realizing that you learn how to love from them. "Even when they are cranky at the end of the day," Janet said, "they say 'Thank you for putting up with me.'"

Mentoring is one of the most important ways in which God calls youth and young adults *through* adults. During my teen years I was mentored by a woman, though I was not aware of it at the time. Sister Theresita encouraged me to volunteer as a teacher at a residential center for mentally and physically handicapped children, and invited me to teach students one-on-one who were preparing to receive communion. She even had me driving her around the state to conferences and meetings on religious education for special needs children. Without my even knowing it, she mentored me into the world of residential and home-based care; she let me see the impoverished and biased attitudes of people; and she let me experience what children with special needs could learn about the faith and teach me.

Mentors are adults in the wider world through whom young people seek recognition (who I am) and a glimpse of a meaningful future (what I can give my life for). Mentoring, according to Sharon Daloz Parks, is "an intentional, mutually demanding, and meaningful relationship between two individuals, a young adult and an older, wiser figure who assists the young person in learning the ways of life." Parks suggests that "mentoring" be used in this specific sense, reserved for those who have a "distinctive role in the story of human becoming." Parents are not necessarily mentors. Obviously parents are crucial for forming an identity, but mentors point to the need for other adults in young people's lives to help them find their way.

Mentors play many roles. They offer support, give resources, and comfort; they challenge—gently—and raise critical questions; they are inspiring in the way they live their life; they encourage dialogue to help young persons "make sense" of their experiences. The key to being a good mentor is to resist the temptation to make a young person into "our image." The calling *through* the mentor is to help a person become who the person is called to be. A mentor cares about the other's vocation as a gift from God.

Parks reports that young people, in fact, have their most positive learning experiences in a group of peers with an adult. She advocates creating mentoring environments and communities that help young people create a "network of belonging" in which together they can pose the "big-enough questions" of adult life and dream worthy dreams.

Adults and elders need mentors too, companions and peers that can help them move through the transitions of life with meaning and purpose. Rosie, a ninety-four-year-old woman, had to move into assisted living, giving up her longtime home of fifty years. Janet and Weldon, two residents of the care facility, greeted her the first day and asked her to come to lunch with them. "I was so relieved," Rosie said. "I couldn't imagine going to the dining room alone and figuring it all out. Here were two angels come to greet me!" Making one's way in a new environment requires the help of others. The care facility did not have a mentoring program, and Janet and Weldon probably did not think they were mentoring. But as fellow travelers, they recognized another's need and responded with care and concern, ready to show Rosie the way on a new path.

How might others be called by God *through* you?

"In Christ Jesus you are all children of God through faith." (Galatians 3:26)

It might be safe to say that Paul's favorite preposition is "through." God has worked through Christ to undo our sinfulness: "For since death came through a human being, the resurrection of the dead has also come *through* a human being" (1 Cor. 15:21). He praises God for what comes through Christ: "Therefore, since we are justified by faith, we have peace with God *through* our Lord Jesus Christ" (Rom. 5:1).

Paul recognizes that the Spirit of the risen Christ continues to work through us: "God's love has been poured into our hearts *through* the Holy Spirit that has been given to us" (Rom. 5:5). For Paul, God has work to do through each of us for the good of all of us: "So we are ambassadors for Christ, since God is making his appeal *through* us" (2 Cor. 5:20).

If the church is to be a community of disciples, it also needs to be a school of mentoring and vocation. Jack Fortin writes, "I believe that congregations are the best places for God's people to be inspired and equipped to live out their callings every day. I envision congregations as places where people gather, are cared for, equipped and validated for their everyday mission and ministry and then set free to serve God in their many vocational settings." What can you do to help your community be agents of God's call *through* you to others?

CHAPTER 7

Called in Suffering

———

"O my God, I cry by day, but you do not answer;
and by night, but find no rest." (Psalm 22:2)

The truth about vocation is that it does not always involve choice or movement. It is not always about going
to or *from*. Sometimes it is about figuring out God's call
in the place that you are.

Martin Luther is helpful on this point. He lived in
a time when people did not have a choice about jobs
or marriage—for men, if your father was a baker, you
became a baker, and women served in the home. Luther
called this your "station" in life and believed that it is *in*
that station that you are called to love God and neighbor to God's glory. Luther revolutionized vocation by
claiming that God calls *all* Christians, not just the clergy

or religious monks, but *all* the baptized through their daily life. He explained that no calling is higher or better than other callings—they are only distinct from one another.

I'm adopting Luther's insight about being called *in* a situation, not necessarily a station in life, but those times when you have little choice. About the only choice you do have is how to live out your calling *in* the situation. You can find yourself *in* situations that require patience and waiting or duty and obligation. Such situations can entail suffering and pain, not joy and peace, at least not initially. It may not be what you want, or where your gifts lie, but it is in fact where you are. In that place, you ask: God, what are you calling me to *in* this circumstance?

Take, for example, those who have to work in jobs they find meaningless or do not like. It is difficult for them to say: "God called me *to* this and I have such joy!" Most people work to support themselves and their family, or because it is the only work they can find. When Maria and Juan came to the United States from Mexico, Maria was a trained health-care worker, but her credentials did not transfer and she could not find work. Initially she took a job cleaning houses, and eventually she was hired as an aide in an assisted living facility, a position for which she was overqualified. But with small children and Juan's untimely death, she could not afford the time and money to get the "right" credentials. She found herself in jobs she did not particularly like or was called to; she found herself in widowhood and single-parenting; and she found herself in poverty, first in a poor and then in a wealthy country. Does it make sense to talk about Maria's life as having callings when there is not much choice for her?

What is your experience of being in a situation where you had to reevaluate your sense of God's calling and purpose? How have you found God's calling in a situation beyond your choice or control? Did God find you in that place?

"My God, my God, why have you forsaken me?"
(Psalm 22:1)

When Jerry left his boss's office, he was numb. He couldn't believe it—he'd been fired after two years on the job. It wasn't as though everything was perfect about the job, but he didn't know it was bad enough to be let go. He was so angry at his boss—why didn't anyone tell him things were not going well? "I always wondered if it was this woman, Sandy, who did me in—I know she never liked me. I felt angry and hurt by the company but I also felt really embarrassed. How was I going to tell my wife or, worse yet, my father, who thinks I'm successful? Was there something I did wrong and didn't know it?"

Jerry was shocked into numbness and disbelief; he was angry and felt betrayed. Most of us receive bad news this way. At first we don't believe it. We reject and deny that it is happening. We blame someone else. Did we do something to cause this? It is quite normal to turn these emotions toward God. Anna heaped all her wrath onto God when she was diagnosed with Lou Gehrig's disease. "I hated God," she said. "For months after my diagnosis of ALS, I couldn't go to church, or listen to anyone tell me that 'God only gives us what we can handle.' That was not a God I wanted to know. I was losing everything in my life as I'd known it. If God gave me this disease thinking I can handle it, God was wrong."

For Jews and Christians, the psalms of lament are the best biblical source for fighting with God in a situation not of our own choosing. The psalmist gives voice to our agony and terror of suffering:

My God, my God, why have you forsaken me?

to our shame:

> But I am a worm, and not human;
> scorned by others, and despised by the people;

and to our fears:

> Many bulls encircle me,
> strong bulls of Bashan surround me;
> they open wide their mouths at me,
> like a ravening and roaring lion.
>
> (Ps. 22:1, 6, 12–13)

Walter Brueggemann, a scholar of the Hebrew Bible, points out that the psalms are not God speaking to us but the common voice of humanity speaking to God. Laments give voice to our profound disorientation, the loss of a world of promise and goodness. The loss of the promise of a calling and purpose.

"I could not get off the couch. I sat watching old movies, searching the Web for sports stories, and ate too much crap. I was getting depressed and drinking too much as well," Jerry says. "I just couldn't get going. Looking for a new job was scary—I didn't want to face losing a job again, but I needed money and had to find some work."

―――

"In you our ancestors trusted;
they trusted, and you delivered them." (Psalm 22:4)

Gradually, over time, you live beyond the initial shock and live into the situation. The unbearable becomes a truth you can admit and name: "I got fired." "I have cancer." "My husband has Alzheimer's." The situation becomes the "new normal." Anna realized that her disease was progressive, that over time she would lose capacity, but not overnight. "I began to see that 'okay, I have ALS, but I am not ALS.' Today this is what I can do. I had to stop worrying about all that was going to happen when I become debilitated and find what I could do today. Even though the range has narrowed, I do have some control over some things." Jerry too realized that he had to take the next step. "One day I just had to stop sitting around feeling pathetic. I got up and started searching the Web for job positions. I couldn't be without work forever—I needed to get going. But I also needed to get out of the rut I was digging myself into."

In suffering, you become angry and reject God. But eventually, if you stay with the anger and abandonment, if you heap your sorrow onto God, you begin searching for God in the place you are, not where you'd like to be. You may think that it is not faithful to be angry with God or to scream at God about what is unfair and painful, but the lament psalms show us that this is prayer—you direct your feelings from the situation you are in to God. In the Christian story, Jesus used the words of Psalm 22 to express his despair as he was enduring his execution, torture, and death. He implored God, "Why have you forsaken me?" (Matt. 27:46), crying out the same words his Jewish ancestors had prayed. These texts have held a prominent place in the Christian tradition precisely because they connect people who lament before God across the ages.

The lament psalms show you a way of being in relationship with God even when God seems absent and silent, when the ways you are used to being with God become empty and hollow, and when God does not seem to be rescuing you from your misery. Does this God save or not? You may wonder—is God punishing me for something I did, or is God testing me to see if I am strong? Many people who experience profound suffering finally give up on a God who punishes or tests them because it does not make much sense that an all-loving God would manipulate human persons into obedience and faith. Part of the suffering in suffering is reexamining our notions about God. We are shocked when God doesn't deliver what we want. "I begged

God every day, and then I reminded God that he is God and should act like it! I even bargained with God, promising to go to church if I could just get through this," Maria said.

The lament psalms name the profound disorientation that comes from loss, disaster, and suffering. But they also speak of reorientation: a new kind of faith that is not simple or simplistic, not resigned or passive, but something new. In suffering, you can move from seeking explanations about God to finding God, discovering that faith is not belief in a set of ideas about who God is and how God operates, but trust that God remains with you and you remain with God, no matter your circumstances. For many the insight that God never abandons them despite their misery pushes their faith to a new place. For Jesus, it meant giving himself over in death, trusting in God's goodness and mercy such that at his death, he was able to pray the words "Into your hands I commend my spirit" (Luke 23:46).

~~~~~

"Caminemos con Jesús—
Let us walk with Jesus!"

Maria, too, had to learn that God was not a miracle worker in the way she wanted, but that another kind of miracle was happening in her life and through her struggles. She was learning what it means to live every day trusting in God as a partner and friend. "I finally came to realize that God was not at my beck and call to do what I wanted. And maybe God was not a miracle worker, either, at least not the way I wanted. I was sitting in church one day and we were singing and in that moment I realized that God was calling me to walk the path that Jesus walked, even though I didn't want to and didn't know the way. Jesus seemed to be saying to me: Trust me, come along with me."

Many Mexican American Christians on Good Friday sing a litany that speaks of this trust: "*Caminemos con Jesús*—Let us walk with Jesus." For the poor, the immigrant, the sick, and the stranger, the Gospels reveal that those who walk with Jesus in his suffering become a community of disciples, able to walk with one another in suffering. The Gospel writers link Jesus with the figure of the Suffering Servant from the book of Isaiah,

declaring Jesus as a participant in the suffering of inno-
cent victims. Through Jesus, Maria and her community
are not called to be victimized by their suffering, but are
called to walk with one another in suffering.

When faith turns from understanding to trust, God
is revealed as our companion in suffering, not the cause
or the cure of suffering. Gerald Calhoun, a chaplain to
the chronically ill, says people travel a road that can take
them "from seeing God as enemy, to meeting an absent
God, and eventually to discovering a God who is a companion and renews their life." If you engage with God,
even in prayers of lament, you stay in relationship, and
relationships grow and change over time if both parties are invested. If you stay engaged, questioning and
searching, being honest in the situation, Calhoun says,
you will eventually "meet a God [you] can trust." Jerry
said, "I sat moaning to my friends, my wife, and my
family for a long time. A few years later I realized how
important it was that they walked with me through the
anger and pain. They knew I was lost but believed that
I could find my way. I came to realize that God was one
of those friends too."

In the midst of lament, telling God his story, the
psalmist recalls other times in life when God was present. The psalmist remembers God's goodness for the
community in the past:

Yet you are holy,
> enthroned on the praises of Israel.
In you our ancestors trusted;
> they trusted, and you delivered them.
To you they cried, and were saved;
> in you they trusted, and were not put to shame.

(Ps. 22:3–5)

The psalmist is mindful that this present suffering is not the whole story, nor is it God's intention for the people. In fact, the God who has been with them since birth is the same God who is seeking them in life.

The journey of suffering entails finding a meaning and purpose *in* your situation. It means searching beyond what happened to you or why it happened, to ask, "What does this situation mean for my life, for our lives? Who am I now? How can I live given the situation I am *in?*" In terms of vocation, "What is God's call *in* this place?" Anna said, "I had to discover that a part of my life had ended. It was over, but my life was not finished. I was still living. I had to live as fully as possible given what I can do and be. Living with ALS is a cat-and-mouse game. Some days I feel fine; other days I'm awful; some seasons are good, others I'm failing. That's just the way it is and I don't have a lot of control over it. I had to give up my desire to control my disease and find a way to choose what I could change and do, and a lot of that was my attitude. I have to find that every day." If vocation is God's call in our situation, we might wake up to the reality that God is searching for us at the same time we are searching for God. We may never find an answer to why we suffer, but we may find meaning in it.

In another popular song in the Hispanic Christian community, the people sing, "Lord, you have looked into my eyes; smiling, you have called my name." God may be calling us to new insights, acceptance, or a new way of being in the world. God may be calling us to take up new work and service. God may be blessing us with new gifts and capacities. "I've become more patient," Jerry said. Anna says, "On good days I am able to make prayer shawls and baby quilts for new mothers." And Maria has found she can serve as a nurse's aid with joy, but only after she rooted out bitterness from her heart. In small ways, these people have found a way to give their life in service to others despite their situation and yet in it.

*"He did not hide his face from me,
but heard when I cried to him."* (Psalm 22:24)

Out of the despair of loss—of jobs, roles, homes, physical abilities—many people keep on living, finding purpose and meaning. In fact, the psalmist never states that God makes everything better or returns our life to what it had been before. Rather, the psalmist proclaims faith in a God who never hides, abandons, or forgets. The divine Holy Mystery is always and everywhere present, particularly seeking out those who are weak and vulnerable, those who suffer innocently, and those who bear great pain. God, then, is more like a nurse or a midwife than a magician, offering care and compassion for our health and well-being; God is like a friend, walking alongside and listening; God is a confidant, holding us while we plead and cry.

Great suffering can push us to relinquish false hope for a true hope. Hope, in the midst of suffering, begins with a basic realism that things are what they are and that, in the many valleys of our lives, God is present as a comfort and a guide. Hope is the capacity to look *in* our present circumstances and see what is possible; it is also the capacity to look beyond ourselves to a time of greater wholeness, in this life as well as beyond our earthly life. Jerry found another job that he enjoys. Maria found a way to volunteer at school and help kids struggling with English. Anna found that while she hopes for a cure for ALS, she can't sit and wait for that to happen, at least not in her lifetime: "I had to find hope in my life now, in what I can do and what I can be. I found that hope is both a way of seeing the world and also a feeling of being alive for something more." Hope can only make sense when it is linked to faith and love. Jesus teaches us to hope for wholeness, peace, and goodness because in our suffering we grow to trust God, the one who makes us whole through love. And as we walk with Jesus, we share his hope in the One who transforms suffering and death into new life.

"Standing near the cross of Jesus were his mother, and his mother's sister ... and Mary Magdalene ... and the disciple whom he loved." (John 19:25–26)

If God calls you in your suffering and pain, God is also calling you to accompany those who suffer and who die. All disciples are called to be compassionate to those who suffer, to "suffer with" them, as the term implies. Jesus felt that he was abandoned by God and the disciples, but in John's Gospel those that he calls "friends" become the community that gathers at the foot of his cross. His friends do not abandon him, staying with him through his suffering and death; they are called to give their lives to accompany one another through the water and blood that pour forth from his side (John 19:34).

Have you been a caregiver or do you know a caregiver? According to former First Lady Rosalynn Carter, the answer is yes. She says, "There are only four kinds of people in the world: those who have been caregivers, those who are currently caregivers, those who will be caregivers, and those who will need caregivers." Caregiving is part of all human life—the care for children, the sick, the elderly, and the dying. Often you don't choose caregiving—it chooses you. A spouse is ill or a parent needs your help or a child is born with special needs, and you find yourself, quite suddenly at times, *in* a situation you did not plan or want.

A study conducted by the Rosalynn Carter Institute found that 80 percent of caregivers are women, 61 percent are married, a third have been giving care for ten or more years, 41 percent spend more than forty hours a week caregiving, and 50 percent report being burned out. Tom has had Alzheimer's disease for about ten years, and Betty has cared for him in their home up to now. "At first, it was not bad. He was just Tom, a little forgetful, but he could do most things he wanted. Now he is barely able to care for himself and I have to do most everything. I know he is more than the disease but some days it just seems like all I do is wash, cook, feed, clean up, and then do it all over again."

Caregivers experience isolation, and struggle to ask others for help. In the study cited above, 75 percent of caregivers said they provide all or most of the care; 50 percent turn to family for help, but of these, nearly 66 percent receive no or little help. Only 16 percent of survey respondents turned to outside agencies for help. While caregivers accompany someone who needs their help, there are few companions who accompany them. "My daughters stop by and help me on the weekends," Betty said, "but most of the week we are alone in the house. We used to eat out, but Tom has a hard time getting into the car and is confused when we leave the house."

Caregivers experience their own losses, including loss of income, leisure time, freedom, privacy, companionship, and sex. Though they struggle to say it, life has significantly changed for them, and resentment of a loved one's dependence—compounded by a sense of guilt over the resentment—rises up. They fear the death of their loved one as they watch him or her change and decline over time. "I don't know what I'll do when Tom goes, but I also hope this does not go on forever," Betty said. "I've been really blessed to be able to care for Tom, and most every day I feel like God and my family have sustained me through this. I couldn't do it without them."

Caregiving, many people say, is the hardest calling they have had to respond to. Most would not choose it if they had a choice. Some experience it as God's calling, some do not. But regardless, they discover something *in* caregiving. Caregivers can also experience positive changes in their lives: they may become more understanding of others' needs, more sympathetic, compassionate, sensitive, and aware. They may develop stronger coping and listening skills, self-preservation, and personal values. As they gain responsibility, they can let go of being scared or depressed. Many become grateful over time.

To care is to accompany another on the other's journey, even the journey to death. Accompanying the dying can sharpen your callings. Jolene, who was focused on her work and career, found a new calling from God when a friend was diagnosed with cancer. She became involved in the Race for the Cure, served on its board for many years, volunteered at a hospice, and has cared for her sick father. It was her friend's illness and eventual dying that changed the course of her life. In the face of death, caregivers become the friends who sit at the foot of the cross, in faith and sadness, not in despair or isolation. Henri Nouwen writes, "To care for others as they become weaker and closer to death is to allow them to fulfill their deepest vocation, that of becoming ever-more fully what they already are: daughters and sons of God."

You may at times find yourself in a place not of your own choosing. Don't hesitate to ask God: "What is my calling in this place? Let me know—soon, please."

CHAPTER 8

Called by the God **Within**

$$\overline{}$$

"The kingdom of God is within you." (Luke 17:21)

God's callings can come to you in many ways—through others, through recognizing your gifts in service and work that make a difference for others, in your sorrows and pain, and at times in your dreams. But the call *within* takes some effort on your part. You have to attend to and build your capacity to listen to the One who dwells *within* you.

The preposition "within" points to two great mysteries of the Christian faith—God comes to dwell *within* our midst, abiding *within* us, and God calls each of us to abide *within* the One Holy Mystery. The call *within* is God's sheer graced goodness, a gift of pure love, a boundless power that is our source and destiny.

But how? The call *within* is often difficult to hear because of the many distractions that keep you from listening to this source. How do you cultivate your awareness of the divine presence *within* you? How do you pray and listen?

"How lovely is your dwelling place, O LORD of hosts!"
(Psalm 84:1)

The story of God's dwelling place is told throughout the Christian narrative. In the Hebrew Bible, the Israelites, once freed from slavery, wander in the desert, seeking a home, searching for the Promised Land. Over those forty years they experienced the Holy One dwelling in their midst, through cloud and manna, and eventually the ark. "You shall offer the passover sacrifice to the LORD your God, from the flock and the herd, at the place that the LORD will choose as a dwelling for his name" (Deut. 16:2). When they came into the land, the mount of Jerusalem and the temple became God's dwelling place, and people journeyed from afar to sing God's praises in that place:

How lovely is your dwelling place,
　O LORD of hosts! (Ps. 84:1)

Once the land and the temple were lost and the people were forced into exile, they clung to the promise that God did not leave them forsaken to their enemies. The prophet Ezekiel comforts the exiles by pronouncing that God is with them wherever they are: "My dwelling place shall be with them; and I will be their God, and they shall be my people" (Ezek. 37:27). The people come to recognize that God dwells *with* them:

Lord, you have been our dwelling place
　in all generations. (Ps. 90:1)

In the Christian story Jesus is declared to be God's dwelling place. When Jesus calls the disciples at the beginning of John's Gospel, they ask him, "Where are you staying?" He replies, "Come and see" (John 1:39). Of course, they want to see his house, but he invites them on a journey to discover that he is the dwelling place of the Most High. He says seven times in John's Gospel, "I am," echoing Moses's conversation about God's name. Jesus identifies his unity with the Holy One by revealing that he is the "bread of life," the "light of the world," the "gate," the "good shepherd," the "resurrection and the life," the "way, the truth and the life," the "vine." Through these powerful images Jesus reveals that the dwelling place of the Holy Presence is *within* him.

But the disciples do not always understand what is right in front of them. When the three disciples encounter Jesus's transfiguration, Peter immediately wants to build a site on the mountain: "Lord, it is good for us to be here; if you wish, I will make three dwellings." But Jesus does not intend to stay on a mountaintop in a new house; rather, he means to descend the mountain and follow the path of his calling. And he intends for the disciples to do the same—Jesus assures the disciples that God's dwelling is *within* him, and those who follow him find their dwelling *within* God: "As the Father has loved me, so I have loved you; abide in my love" (John 15:9). And Paul challenges the early Christians to see their bodies as the dwelling place of God: "Do you not know that your body is a temple of the Holy Spirit within you, which you have from God, and that you are not your own?" (1 Cor. 6:19). How do you experience the God who dwells within you?

—————

"Contemplation is also the response to a call:
a call from Him who has no voice, yet Who speaks
in everything that is." (Thomas Merton)

Michaelina was wondering how she might pray differently during the season of Lent. She got an idea from a Sunday sermon. "Turn off your radio in the car," the pastor suggested. That sounded easy enough. "So I turned my radio off the first morning and it was not so bad, but I got fidgety. I wanted to know the weather or what was going on. I couldn't really figure out what to do with silence." In the next few weeks, the silence allowed her to pray. "I had a few conversations with God, asking God to help somebody at work, to watch over my father-in-law, who was sick, and to help my son get a job. I just rattled on and on. But then I realized I was doing all the talking. I was just filling up the silence. If I wanted to listen, I needed to shut up! Eventually, I realized that I would not turn the radio back on after Easter. I could not let go of this silence—I just wanted to be with God in this quiet place."

God's first language, according to Saint John of the Cross, a sixteenth-century mystic, is silence, a language that is beyond human words. Some encounters with

God defy speech, and words must be abandoned. In the Christian tradition, this kind of prayer is called contemplative prayer and includes those practices in which our prayer is wordless, even without thought, when we open ourselves to the silence *within*. In our silence, God is present in God's silent, loving embrace; we can come to know God beyond any knowledge, or words, about God. We know through love. As Thomas Keating, a founding member of Contemplative Outreach, says, "Through grace we open our awareness to God whom we know by faith is within us, closer than breathing, closer than thinking, closer than choosing, closer than consciousness itself."

After not securing a full-time teaching position, Diane was struggling to figure out what was next in her life. She was hoping a one-week silent retreat would help her discern what was next.

After six days of sitting in silent meditation for over eight hours a day, and honoring a commitment to not talk or read the rest of the time, I experienced a profound sense of internal quiet. Yet, I must confess, I was disappointed as I approached the last day of the retreat. I had hoped to receive guidance regarding where God was calling me next.

One evening, in the chapel, I gazed upon an icon of Jesus standing on the shore extending his hand to two apostles disembarking from their boat. I pleaded: "How are You extending your hand to me?" I closed my eyes and looked within. My thoughts turned to conversations I was having with different people, in places I didn't recognize. I noticed all kinds of creative possibilities, beyond the constraints of the traditional kind of teaching I had been doing. And I heard three words: "partners in production." I had no idea what these three words meant. Who were these partners? What production? How would I find them or how would they find me? I had hoped for a more clear-cut direction from my time in silence, and yet, I was intrigued. I was being invited to something more. And yet, I was being asked to trust that this new invitation would reveal itself over time.

Have you felt the call to silence? To contemplative prayer? It is not a practice for the spiritual elite. It is the invitation to pay attention to the silence *within* yourself. It takes your effort to seek out God, to silence your mind's rumblings, and to wait. What you discover is that God is already dwelling within you, calling you to dwell within the divine holy presence. Silence has the capacity to unmask what is false inside you, peeling layer upon layer of your self-absorption away, and remaking you into the image of Christ, the one who empties himself in loving service (Phil. 2:7). The fruit of dwelling in silence is to purify your heart in order that you can trust and be ready to respond to God's call as it unfolds in time. Contemplative prayer purifies your intentions. Over time, as Cynthia Bourgeault notes, you do not go to contemplative prayer as much as "it becomes more and more a place you come from."

"The word . . . is in your mouth and in your heart."
(Deuteronomy 30:14)

Of course, the other language God uses is words: God is waiting to encounter you when you read and listen to the words of Scripture. John begins his Gospel declaring "In the beginning was the Word, and the Word was with God, and the Word was God. . . . And the Word became flesh and lived among us" (John 1:1, 14). After Jesus's death and resurrection, the early community was called to spread the word, the good news of what God had done through Christ. Guided by the work of the

Spirit, they began telling the story of Jesus, and eventually some began to write it down. The written word, the collection of writings that eventually became the Bible, is proclaimed when we gather together for fellowship and worship. God's Word is alive and living among us and *within* us.

The way that early Christians put the Word of God in their mouths and in their hearts was by memorizing Scripture, often a word or a phrase at a time. The psalms were the primary texts they memorized, since the psalms capture a full range of human experience and are prayers of praise, thanksgiving, joy, grief, sadness, and lament. What happens when the words of Scripture become part of your daily consciousness, replacing the words of your scattered thoughts and wandering minds?

I found that by repeating the psalms over and over, they begin to read me. I was memorizing Psalm 1, a simple, short psalm that contrasts the life of the good with the way of the wicked (an ancient motif in the Bible's wisdom literature). Of course, I don't see myself on the side of the wicked, at least not as expressed in the first line: "Happy are those who do not follow the advice of the wicked," or in the second line, "or take the path that sinners tread." But as I repeated the third line—"or sit in the seat of scoffers"—I was hit between the eyes. I had to admit to myself, "I'm a scoffer." I sit on the sidelines and judge what other people are doing, sometimes deriding them. Scoffers, I realized, are people who tear down community; they do not build it up. The text pointed to a real situation in my life, the lunch table at work, where I was scoffing too much and from which I had to walk away.

While Psalm 1 helped me see a side of myself I didn't want to admit, it also gave me an image of what God was calling me to:

> They [the righteous] are like trees
>> planted by streams of water,
> which yield their fruit in its season.
>
> (Ps. 1:3)

Here were two clear paths I could choose: sitting on the scoffers' bench or being a tree of bountiful fruit. The proclamation of God's Word, then, does not tell you only what happened long ago, but it "reads" you in your present life and calls you to change your ways.

"Keep death daily before your eyes."

God's callings encompass your whole life, your whole life long: who you are, how you live, and what you do. But the particular callings that constitute your life come to an end. Most of your callings are bound by time and place. Vocation is temporal: your particular callings are not eternal or permanent. And yet God promises an eternal vocation beyond your earthly existence.

Dying is a part of life's journey. "Keep death daily before your eyes," teaches Saint Benedict. He did not mean this to be morbid, but as a teaching that gives your life meaning and focus. We've all heard the saying—"live as if today were your last day"—but that seems to be saying something quite different, like do something amazing. To remember your death daily means to live more deeply into the life you have been given and the callings that encompass your life—the ones you have chosen and the ones that have chosen you.

Can you be called in and beyond your dying? Henri Nouwen writes, "Dying is the most general human event, something we all have to do. But do we do it well? Is our death more than an unavoidable fate that we simply wish would not be? Can it somehow become an act of fulfillment, perhaps more human than any other human act?" After an accident, in which he had to be cared for like a child, Nouwen experienced the vulnerability of needing to be cared for by others. "All at once, I knew that all human dependencies are embedded in a divine dependence and that that divine dependence makes dying part of a greater and much vaster way of living." To be called to die, and to be called in your dying, may in fact be the greatest act of faith and trust God asks of you.

You prepare to die as you prepare to live. If your life has been lived in relation *to* God and *for* others, then dying becomes a calling *within* God. As Nouwen notes, "dying becomes the way to everlasting fruitfulness. Here is the most hope-giving aspect of death. Our death may be the end of our success, our productivity, our fame, or our importance among people, but it is not the end of our fruitfulness." The way you have lived out your multiple callings continues through lives you have touched and influenced, the work you have been able to do, the service you have given and received.

At many Christian funerals, a white cloth, called a "pall," is placed over the casket. It is a symbol of baptism and Christ's resurrection. Just as you wore a white gown at your baptism, symbolizing your new life in Christ, you are dressed again in a garment symbolizing yet another dying and rising in Christ. We are reminded again that our eternal calling began before we were formed in the womb (Jer. 1:5) and continues in the "unending, ever-deepening communion" with God, as Nouwen says, a life *within* God beyond death: the calling to "dwell in the house of the LORD my whole life long" (Ps. 23:6).

CHAPTER 9

Callings All **around** Us

We are called
by God;
to be followers, worshipers, witnesses, neighbors,
forgivers, prophets, and stewards;
as the community we are, in the particularity
of our context;
from our losses to a new life together;
for each other and for God's world;
through each other as agents of God's calling;
in our suffering; and
within God's dwelling place.

If you want to hear a good story, ask people about their callings. God's callings are all around us. Many people have never been asked, "What is God calling you to in your life?" Like Jay, whose story I shared at the outset of this book, we are *living* vocation, but we do not tell the stories we live as calling stories.

Why share our stories with each other? Because storytelling builds bonds of trust; it is the foundation of community. Storytelling requires two things. First is the ability to listen to yourself, discern God's holy presence in your life, and share that story with others. Second is listening attentively to another's story. As you listen, you can be captured by stories that are similar to your experience. You can feel a commonality with another. This is called *sympathy*—we resonate with what it is like to "walk in another's shoes." Whose story in this book resonated with you?

We can also realize that other people's lives are quite different from our own. Francois's story is not my story. He is from Burkina Faso, a small nation in West Africa. He left at the age of twenty-six to migrate to the United States looking for work as a sociologist. He never found a job in his field. He began washing dishes in a restaurant and eventually took up cooking and baking. He lost everything and had to start over again. It is hard for me to sympathize with his story since mine is so different, but I can *empathize*. Empathy is the ability to enter into stories that are radically different from your experience. You have to imagine what it is like to go through an event in another person's life, to intuit what the other felt, and to understand how the other views it. Stories awaken you to experiences not your own; this enlarges your world and draws you deeper into relationship with others. Whose stories in this book are different from yours and invite your empathy?

I've shared many stories in this book because I believe vocation is best understood in the stories we live. My understanding of calling changed because of all the stories I've heard. My own sense of calling also changed through the stories I told from my life. I have a high antenna now for calling stories. I hope the stories I have shared can guide you in naming God's callings in your life—if you look, they are all around you.

Reflection Questions

For small-group discernment;
for conversations with family, friends, or work colleagues;
or for individual prayer

BY

» Recollect a time when you felt God at work in your life. What did you learn from this experience?
» Consider your callings: Are they like the acorn, the pilgrimage, or a surprising discovery? What other images of God and vocation come to mind from your callings?

TO

» How have you experienced God's call to be a follower, worshiper, witness, neighbor, forgiver, prophet, and steward? What features stand out in your life?

» How do you experience multiple callings in your life?

AS

» What are the particular contexts of your life? How do these contexts shape your sense of your callings?

» How did you experience callings in childhood or as a youth? How do you experience God's callings at this age in your life?

FROM

» What has God called you from?

» Where did this calling lead you?

FOR

» What gives you great joy? What are your gifts?

» Who needs your gifts, service, and work?

THROUGH

» Who has been an agent of God's calling for you?

» Who are you called to be an agent for?

» How might your community become a community of calling?

IN

» In what situations have you struggled to hear God's call?

» What have you learned about your callings in times of suffering?

WITHIN

» What practices might help you cultivate a sense of God's calling within?

» How might you live so as to prepare to die?

Acknowledgments

The stories in this book have been drawn from research conducted by the Collegeville Institute Seminars, an interdisciplinary, ecumenical, collaborative research project that gathers ordained and lay ministers, theologians, philosophers, psychologists, historians, ethicists, and sociologists to study important questions facing Christians today. As we began this research, we launched small groups in congregations to explore the notion of God's call in their lives. We facilitated groups that met for up to six sessions, through two programs— *Called to Life* (www.called-to-life.com) and *Called to Work* (www.called-to-work.com). We've listened to hundreds of people in the past several years. I use many of these stories throughout the book, but have changed people's names. I also use stories from a series of video narratives, *Lives Explored*, which we developed to showcase stories of vocation (www.lives-explored.com). You are welcome to use these resources for education, worship, or personal reflection. I want to thank the many people who shared their stories with us.

I also want to thank the members of two Collegeville Institute Seminars for their thorough and engaging work on vocation. The Seminar on Vocation and Faith in the Professions is working on articulating the relationship between professions and vocation, the focus of the chapter "Called *for* Service and Work." A second group, the Seminar on Vocation across the Lifespan, is studying how God's call is experienced and lived from childhood to old age, discussed in the chapter "Called *as* We Are."

I am grateful to many colleagues who gave me valuable input on this book and some stories to share as well: residents and staff at Studium at Saint Benedict's Monastery, where I spent a year's sabbatical; Shirley Roels, director of NetVUE (Network on Vocation in Undergraduate Education); John Lewis and Jane Patterson, codirectors of the Workshop in San Antonio, Texas; Mary Stimming, for copy editing; Lil Copan from Eerdmans, for editorial direction; Jane Leyden Cavanaugh, our small-group facilitator; and Diane Millis, producer of *Lives Explored*. I am especially grateful to Laura Kelly Fanucci, the Seminar's research associate and author of *Called to Life* and *Called to Work*, who has been an invaluable conversation partner, editor, coauthor, and companion in this work.

I am also grateful to Craig Dykstra and Chris Coble, program officers at Lilly Endowment, Inc., for their generous financial support of this project and their longtime commitment to fostering Christian understandings of vocation.

Finally, I am deeply grateful to the Collegeville Institute for hosting our research project. The Institute seeks to discern the meaning of Christian identity and unity in a religiously and culturally diverse world, and to communicate that meaning for the work of the church and the renewal of human community. The Institute practices first-person storytelling out of the conviction that every Christian is a theologian and has something to say about God. It has embraced this method since its inception in the 1960s. This method assumes that all good theology, however scholarly, has the weight of lived faith beneath and within it. This method allowed Christians to tell the stories of their faith lives across denominational boundaries at a time when the churches held mostly prejudicial and narrow views of one another. For more information about the Collegeville Institute's programs, including the seminars and a description of the first-person method, go to http://collegevilleinstitute.org.

References

CHAPTER 1

The biblical quotations in this book come from the New Revised Standard Version.

The images of the acorn and the journey are drawn from Marie Theresa Coombs and Francis Kelly Nemeck, *Called by God: A Theology of Vocation and Lifelong Commitment* (Eugene, OR: Wipf and Stock, 2001), pp. 32-33.

For the story of walking the Camino de Santiago to Santiago de Compostela in Spain, see Arthur Paul Boers, *The Way Is Made by Walking* (Downers Grove: InterVarsity, 2007); quotation from p. 26.

Ken's story is featured in one of our video interviews at www .lives-explored.com.

CHAPTER 2

The seven features of discipleship spoken of in this chapter—to be a follower, a worshiper, a witness, a neighbor, a forgiver, a prophet, and a steward—are explored in greater depth in a book I coauthored with Laura Kelly Fanucci, *Living Your Discipleship: Seven Ways to Express Your Deepest Calling* (New London, CT: Twenty-Third Publications, 2015).

Sherice's story is told in our video interviews at www .lives-explored.com.

Dorothy's story is recounted in Dorothy C. Bass, "Camping," in Dorothy C. Bass, Kathleen A. Cahalan, Bonnie J. Miller-McLemore, James R. Nieman, and Christian B. Scharen, *Christian Practical Wisdom: What It Is, Why It Matters* (Grand Rapids: Eerdmans, 2016), p. 66.

Angela's story is told in our video interviews at www.lives -explored.com.

For the quotation from Jack Fortin, see his *The Centered Life* (Minneapolis: Augsburg Fortress, 2006), p. 15.

John A. Neafsey is a psychologist in Chicago who works with victims of torture and abuse. His book is *A Sacred Voice Is Calling: Personal Vocation and Social Conscience* (Maryknoll, NY: Orbis, 2006); quotations at p. 3.

For the story of Parker Palmer, see his well-known book *Let Your Life Speak: Listening for the Voice of Vocation* (San Francisco: Jossey-Bass, 2000), pp. 4–34.

The three aspects of vocation—who I am, what I do, and how I live—are drawn from Marie Theresa Coombs and Francis Kelly Nemeck, *Called by God: A Theology of Vocation and Lifelong Commitment* (Eugene, OR: Wipf and Stock, 2001), pp. 1–4.

CHAPTER 3

The Edward Hahnenberg quotation comes from his *Awakening Vocation: A Theology of Christian Calling* (Collegeville, MN: Liturgical Press, 2010), p. 139.

The quotation from Joyce Ann Mercer can be found at "Call Forwarding: Putting Vocation in the Present Tense with Youth," *Insights* 123, no. 2 (Spring 2008): 3–12.

I have drawn from Robert Kegan's work on human development in *The Evolving Self* (Cambridge, MA: Harvard University Press, 1982).

The quotation by James W. Fowler is in Dori Grinenko Baker and Joyce Ann Mercer, *Lives to Offer* (Cleveland: Pilgrim Press, 2007), p. 66.

For a discussion of the counternarratives of vocation for youth, see Baker and Mercer, *Lives to Offer*, pp. 25–26.

For an additional resource on youth, vocation, and consumerism, see Katherine Turpin, *Branded: Adolescents Converting from Consumer Faith* (Cleveland: Pilgrim Press, 2006).

The section on vocation and young adults is informed by Sharon Daloz Parks, *Big Questions, Worthy Dreams* (San Francisco: Jossey-Bass, 2000).

Information about late adulthood is drawn from Mary Catherine Bateson, *Composing a Further Life: The Age of Active Wisdom* (New York: Knopf, 2010), pp. 12–13.

For Peg's reflections on retirement, see her video interview at www.lives-explored.com.

CHAPTER 4

The three aspects of life transitions are drawn from William Bridges, *Transitions: Making Sense of Life's Changes* (Cambridge, MA: Da Capo Press, 2004).

For the definition of grief, see Kenneth Mitchell and Herbert Anderson, *All Our Losses, All Our Griefs* (Philadelphia: Westminster, 1983).

The Robert Kegan quotation is from Robert Kegan, *The Evolving Self* (Cambridge, MA: Harvard University Press, 1982), p. 81.

CHAPTER 5

The material from Michael Himes is from his book *Doing the Truth in Love: Conversations about God, Relationships, and Service* (Mahwah, NJ: Paulist, 1995).

For the research on zookeepers, see J. Stuart Bunderson and Jeffery A. Thompson, "The Call of the Wild: Zookeepers, Callings, and the Double-Edged Sword of Deeply Meaningful Work," *Administrative Science Quarterly* 54 (2009): 32–57.

The Greek word *charismata* is a plural form of the noun *charisma*, which is generally translated as "gift." Many words are derived from the Greek root *char*: "joy" is *chara*; "rejoicing" is *chairo*; "thanksgiving" is *eucharista*; "bestowing" is *charizomai*. God's grace is *charis*, a sheer gift that is universal and bestowed on all, whereas *charismata* are particular gifts that flow from grace. See Harley H. Schmitt, *Many Gifts, One Lord* (Minneapolis: Augsburg, 1993), pp. 16ff., 45–49.

Paul advances the idea of charisms in three of his letters: Rom. 12:3–8; 1 Cor. 12:4–11; and Eph. 4:11–16. In each letter he lists a variety of gifts, not in order to create an exhaustive list, but to illustrate the gifts he witnesses in each community and to make a point about their diversity and unity.

On the nature of charisms, gifts, and vocation, I am drawing from conversations with Jane Patterson and John Lewis over the past several years; they generously offered me the quotations for this chapter. You can find out more about their ministry, the Workshop, at http://theworkshop-sa.org/.

See the Gallup report on its annual Work and Education Survey, "The '40-Hour' Workweek Is Actually Longer—by Seven Hours," by Lydia Saad, August 29, 2014, at http://www.gallup.com/poll.175286/hour-work week-actually-longer-seven-hours.aspx.

The quote from Dorothy Sayers is found in Armand Larive, *After Sunday: A Theology of Work* (New York: Continuum, 2004), p. 64.

For the definition and analysis of professions in the American context, see William Sullivan, *Work and Integrity: The Crisis and Promise of Professionalism in America*, 2nd ed. (San Francisco: Jossey-Bass, 2005), pp. 1–18.

CHAPTER 6

The anecdote that opens the chapter comes from Mike Hayes, who recounts his story in his book *Loving Work: A Spiritual Guide to Finding the Work We Love and Bringing Love to the Work We Do* (New York: Orbis, 2012), pp. 37–42.

The quote from Robert Kegan is found on p. 19 in his *The Evolving Self* (Cambridge, MA: Harvard University Press, 1982).

The quotations from Sharon Daloz Parks come from her chapter 8, "The Gifts of a Mentoring Environment," in *Big Questions, Worthy Dreams* (San Francisco: Jossey-Bass, 2000).

The quotation from Jack Fortin comes from his book *The Centered Life* (Minneapolis: Augsburg Fortress, 2006), p. 94.

CHAPTER 7

The Walter Brueggemann material is from his book *The Psalms and the Life of Faith* (Minneapolis: Fortress, 1995).

Gerald Calhoun's quote comes from his book *Pastoral Companionship: Ministry with Seriously-Ill Persons and Their Families* (Mahwah, NJ: Paulist, 1986), p. 30.

For Hispanic theological resources on accompaniment, see Roberto Goizueta, *Caminemos Con Jesús: Toward a Hispanic/Latino Theology of Accompaniment* (Maryknoll, NY: Orbis, 1995), and *Christ Our Companion: Toward a Theological Aesthetics of Liberation* (Maryknoll, NY: Orbis, 2009).

For Rosalynn Carter's insights on caregiving, see *Helping Yourself Help Others: A Book for Caregivers* (New York: Random House, 1994), p. 3.

Henri Nouwen's quotation comes from his book *Our Greatest Gift: A Meditation on Dying and Caring* (New York: Harper-Collins, 1994), pp. 58, 63.

CHAPTER 8

The quotation from Thomas Merton is taken from William Harmless, SJ, "Mystic as Firewalker: Thomas Merton," in *Mystics* (New York: Oxford University Press, 2008), p. 31.

The Thomas Keating quotation comes from the website www.contemplativeoutreach.org/...file/method_cp_eng -2016–06_1.pdf, accessed August 25, 2016. For more on Keating's writings on centering prayer, see http://www .centeringprayer.com/.

The Cynthia Bourgeault quotation comes from her book *Centering Prayer and Inner Awakening* (Lanham, MD: Cowley, 2004), p. 17.

The practice of memorizing psalms comes from the practice of *lectio divina*, "holy reading." For an introduction to *lectio divina*, see Christine Valters Painter and Lucy Wynkoop, *Lectio Divina: Contemplative Awakening and Awareness* (Mahwah, NJ: Paulist, 2008), and Mary Margaret Funk, OSB, *Lectio Matters: Before the Burning Bush* (New York: Continuum, 2010).

For the quotation from *The Rule of Saint Benedict*, see chap. 4, v. 47.

The idea of temporal and eternal calling is taken from Marie Theresa Coombs and Francis Kelly Nemeck, *Called by God: A Theology of Vocation and Lifelong Commitment* (Eugene, OR: Wipf and Stock, 2001), p. 73.

For the Henri Nouwen material, see his book *Our Greatest Gift: A Meditation on Dying and Caring* (San Francisco: HarperOne, 2009), pp. 16, 38.

CHAPTER 9

Francois's story can be heard in our video narratives at www .lives-explored.com.